Endorsements for *Becoming Us*

"Whether you are brand new to the Enneagram or several years into your journey, Jeff and Beth are fantastic mentors throughout the process. Our marriage is better because of them. Studying the McCord's teachings on the Enneagram has given us a deeper appreciation for one another. Once we understand why we do what we do, we can better grow in our relationships with others, especially our spouses. We love how Jeff and Beth always bring it back to the Gospel. Through a personal relationship with Christ, the Enneagram is an effective tool for achieving high levels of marital satisfaction. We highly recommend *Becoming Us* for your marriage."

Ted and Amy Cunningham
Founders, Woodland Hills Family Church
Authors of *Come to the Family Table*

"We have seen firsthand, both in our marriage and in the marriages of countless others, how the Enneagram can bring couples closer, foster empathy, and provide a newfound appreciation for each other's differences. Thank you, Beth and Jeff, for writing *Becoming Us*. Finally, we have a practical and godly tool that can be used to enrich, and even save, many marriages. We can't wait to share it with others."

Gail and Michael Hyatt
Michael Hyatt & Co.

"Beth and Jeff McCord have authored an extraordinary guide for married couples to strengthen the bonds of their friendship and love. Through the Enneagram, couples can gain a greater understanding of each other, and themselves, in a way that is profoundly helpful. Every marriage knows both affection and distance, romance and conflict, the graces of redemption and the curses of the fall. In *Becoming Us*, the McCords pave a well-defined path of hope for both personal and marital growth, and I trust many will benefit from their experience and teaching."

Pastor David Cassidy
Author of *Indispensable* and Lead Pastor, Christ Community Church

"I'm a huge fan of the Enneagram—it's been an extremely useful tool in my life, marriage, and friendships. What I appreciate about the McCord's approach is that it explores the Enneagram through the lens of the Gospel and helps appropriate what the Enneagram is in light of how God made us. This book is equally engaging for newcomers and enthusiasts alike!"

Dave Barnes
Recording artist

"The McCords, using the Enneagram as a tool, have provided a roadmap I wish Les and I had in our early years of marriage, but it's equally relevant to us now as we're still growing and learning, even after 57 years! No matter how long you've been married, *Becoming Us* will give you insight to love each other well."

Patsy Clairmont
Author of *You Are More Than You Know*

"The McCords have written *Becoming Us* as an insightful resource for those who want to understand themselves, their spouse, and their marriage through the lens of faith and the tool of the Enneagram."

Ian Morgan Cron
Author of *The Road Back to You*

"Reading through *Becoming Us* has been helpful for me even as someone who isn't married yet. It's helped me understand not only how to gain better communication skills but how to be more understanding of others who look at life differently than I do. It's definitely helping me be more compassionate and has provided invaluable tools for me to learn to care for others in a more Christlike way."

David Archuleta
Recording artist and *American Idol* runner-up

"We so appreciate Beth and Jeff's helpful and honest approach to marriage in *Becoming Us*. They show us how understanding each other's core fear, desire, weakness, and longings in light of the Gospel can help us communicate with, and love one another, well."

Matt and Lauren Chandler
Matt: author, pastor, president of the Acts 29 Network
Lauren: author, speaker, and singer/songwriter

"Like any tool, the Enneagram can be used correctly or incorrectly, but with the right information and the right teachers, it can be mastered. Through this thoughtful and compassionate book, Beth and Jeff McCord equip couples with exactly what they need to apply the Enneagram exceptionally well—to live and love better. *Becoming Us* will be a precious gift to many."

Ryan O'Neal
Recording artist/Sleeping at Last

"Beth McCord is absolutely one of my favorite voices in the Enneagram world. In *Becoming Us*, she has partnered with her husband, Jeff, to bring their expertise and passion for helping people see Christ using the Enneagram in a new and refreshing way. They are seriously committed to helping relationships thrive. I have been WAITING for this book—so grateful that it is here!"

Annie F. Downs
Author of *100 Days to Brave* and *Remember God*

"As a newlywed couple, the Enneagram has been an essential tool in helping us understand ourselves and each other on a deeper level. Beth and Jeff are the experts we trust for all things Enneagram, and this book is the perfect guide to bring clarity and hope to couples in any stage of life."

George and Whitney Kamel
Host of *The Dave Ramsey Show* video channel & Ramsey Solutions

"The McCords have written a thoroughly Gospel-centered and compelling Enneagram resource for anyone looking for practical ways to better understand and love their spouse. I will be sure to use the insights I have gleaned in my own marriage!"

Bob Osborne
Executive Director at Serge.org

"Biblical marriage is rooted in the intimacy of knowing Jesus and being known by your spouse. Beth and Jeff McCord's teachings on the Enneagram gives us insight into how God has wired us and gives us a greater capacity to be known by others. The truth of the Gospel, along with the Enneagram, make this book a strong tool for strengthening relationships both with the Lord and with others."

Geoff Todd
Director of K-Kauai, Kanakuk Family Kamp

"The Enneagram provides insightful language to help us understand and communicate who we are and why we are this way. *Becoming Us* points to the importance of applying the Gospel as the framework for how these insights can substantially affect both our individual lives and relationships. I'm thankful for how Beth and Jeff beautifully embody the way of Jesus in their teaching and writing."

Curtis Zackery
Author of *Soul Rest* and Pastor, Church of the City

BECOMING *Us*

BECOMING
Us

Using the
Enneagram to Create
a Thriving Gospel-Centered Marriage

BETH McCORD
JEFF McCORD

NASHVILLE

NEW YORK • LONDON • MELBOURNE • VANCOUVER

BECOMING *Us*

Using the Enneagram to Create a Thriving Gospel-Centered Marriage

Published in New York, New York, by Morgan James Publishing. Morgan James is a trademark of Morgan James, LLC. www.MorganJamesPublishing.com

All Scripture quotations, unless otherwise indicated, are taken from The Holy Bible, New International Version®, NIV® or English Standard Version, ESV®.

ISBN 9781642794168 paperback
ISBN 9781642794175 eBook
Library of Congress Control Number: 2018967175

Cover Design by:
Christopher Kirk
www.GFSstudio.com

Jane Butler
Well Refined Creative Director
wellrefined.co

Interior Design by:
Chris Treccani
www.3dogcreative.net

Jane Butler
Well Refined Creative Director
wellrefined.co

Morgan James is a proud partner of Habitat for Humanity Peninsula and Greater Williamsburg. Partners in building since 2006.

Get involved today! Visit
MorganJamesPublishing.com/giving-back

DEDICATION

To Jesus Christ

To our son and daughter, Nathan and Libby

To our parents, Bruce and Dana Pfuetze
and Jerald and Johnny McCord

To our readers

May you come to know the love and care
that you have received from Christ.

Our Mission

"For people to see themselves with astonishing clarity so they can break free from self-condemnation, fear, and shame by knowing and experiencing the unconditional love, forgiveness, and freedom in Christ."

TABLE OF CONTENTS

FOREWORD

"It is *not* good," God said, "for the man to be alone."

Having been married to my wife, Patti, for twenty-four years, I can attest firsthand to the wisdom of God's marriage strategy.

Marriage has been a key influence—second only to Scripture, prayer, and the Triune God—in our character formation. Patti and I have both changed over the years, mostly for the better, and always because of what I call the "sandpaper effect" of our marriage. We began our journey together with some rough, abrasive edges. But as we have rubbed off on each other—sometimes producing a good bit of heat and friction and irritation—the end product has always been something smoother than what was there before.

As we all know, the "sandpaper effect" can also backfire, especially for couples lacking in compassion and empathy toward one another's weaknesses. But when given the right tools to address those weaknesses in a life-giving fashion, we can become more like Jesus: namely, to develop the necessary skills of listening, saying "I'm sorry," granting and receiving forgiveness, and resolving to grow and change for the better.

One tool that has become immensely helpful to Patti and me, and that has equipped us better than perhaps any other tool for our sandpaper moments and seasons, is the Enneagram.

As Jeff and Beth McCord remind us in the first pages of *Becoming Us*, the Enneagram is neither a shield to defend our bad behavior nor a sword to punish the other person. Rather, when properly used, it is a rich resource for understanding the strengths, weaknesses, and opportunities that go along with our respective wirings. Furthermore, it is a resource for moving forward, together, along a more life-giving path.

As we have discovered, Patti is a Type 6 with a 5 wing. On the plus side, this means she is fiercely loyal and deeply curious. However, she can sometimes get tripped up in decision-making, and she can play things way too safe. I, on the other hand, am a Type 3 with a 4 wing. On the plus side, this means I will take creative risks and embark on daring adventures that, while not safe, can yield wonderful payoffs both personally and for the kingdom. However, I can also be prone to telling half-truths instead of the whole truth, make reckless and impulsive decisions, and grow insecure if I sense that people don't like me.

Without going into all the details, our Type 6/3 marriage combination has pushed both Patti and me onto healthier pathways that we would be reluctant to travel on our own. Because of me, her life has become more adventurous and daring. Because of her, my life is more thoughtful and well-balanced than it would be otherwise.

In short, she is better off because of me and I am better off because of her—not in spite of our differences, but precisely because of them.

Without the Enneagram, and without books like *Becoming Us*, I suspect that our awareness of this fact—that our growth into wholeness in Christ depends on the stewardship of our differences—would be much less than it is.

I pray that you would receive Jeff and Beth's insights just as Patti and I do, as wise words from a pastor and an Enneagram Coach who are themselves experienced, healthy, insightful, and daily practitioners of the concepts about which they write. As you immerse yourselves in this book, I trust that you and your spouse will grow in your empathy and appreciation of one another's uniqueness (as well as your own) and that in so doing you will not only grow closer in your marriage but closer to Christ.

Scott Sauls
Pastor of Christ Presbyterian Church in Nashville, Tennessee, Author of *Jesus Outside the Lines* and *Irresistible Faith*

How to Use This Book

When it comes to how people behave, we believe that everyone is actually trying to do the best they can with the information, skills, and tools that are available to them at the time.

That's why Jeff and I love working side by side to help couples understand why they keep veering off course and show them how they can get back on track toward being in healthy alignment in Christ. We listen to struggles, bring clarity to what is happening, and offer guidance from a biblical perspective to help them get back on their best path.

If you are in the position of wanting to get out of the marital rut and quicksand you've fallen into or wanting to figure out why you do the things you do and why your spouse doesn't always seem to "get it," then this is the right place for you.

After all, the purpose of the Enneagram is to awaken *self-awareness* and to provide hope as we look at ourselves and each other. Used properly, it can cut through difficult circumstances to help us understand each other in a more honest and loving way.

But know this: What we offer, including the insights we have learned from scripture and studying the Enneagram, cannot substitute for professional therapy, marriage counseling, or psychological inpatient treatment. We don't intend this book to be a marriage "ICU"!

So, if anything triggers a serious reaction, please don't wait to get help. If you are in a violent or abusive situation, seek help *immediately.* Make sure you are healthy and safe. For a marriage to heal and grow, it must have two healthy partners.

If you're new to the Enneagram, it is sometimes tempting to use what you are learning as either a shield or a sword.

However, the Enneagram is not a shield that we use to defend our behavior, "Well, that's just my Type."

Nor is it a sword to be used to put someone down, "Oh, you're being such a Type __."

Using the Enneagram in this way will only bring more pain and problems to your marriage.

But when used correctly, the Enneagram, as we explain in *Becoming Us,* is designed to help you focus on what's most important: your relationship with God, yourself, and each other.

To make it easy, we've divided *Becoming Us* into two parts. Part 1 is about faith, our story, the Enneagram, and stories about communication and conflict from some friends whose marriages have been impacted by the Gospel and through the Enneagram.

Part 2 is an "Enneagram Roadmap," which is a guide to each of the Types with two parts: how to better understand yourself and how to better understand the Type of your spouse. It is written in a succinct style so you can use it as a handy reference.

We encourage you to read Part 1 first, as it will give you context and explanation for what you'll find on the Enneagram Roadmap, but feel free to flip back and forth as you're learning how it all fits together.

Because no matter where you start, the destination is *Becoming Us.*

Our Kitchen Table

The day was drizzly, cold, and gray, and seemed to match the atmosphere in the hearts of our friends. John and Emily had called and asked to meet with us to talk about where they were struggling in their relationship… they were angry and not communicating well at all. They were, once again, stuck but hoping something could unlock the door to help them relate to each other in ways that didn't involve yelling or shutting down.

John and Emily reached out to us because I'm an Enneagram coach and Jeff is a pastor and mediator. They had heard that we, too, had once been in a very hard place in our marriage and that something had made a drastic impact on, and in, our relationship.

We invited them into our home where we sat around our well-worn kitchen table. After each of us got a cup of coffee (and Emily got a hot tea), we began to talk with them about the two things that radically transformed our relationship with ourselves and with each other: the truth of the Gospel and the Enneagram, an insightful tool that brought astonishing clarity to our hearts' motivations.

The Center of Marriage—the Gospel

Jeff and I have been married for twenty-four years, and we have two grown kids. If asked, I would quickly respond that we are happily married. But before you think that we have it all together and every day is perfect, I want to be very clear and honest with you: "becoming us" hasn't been *easy*.

Truthfully, there have been times when we seemed to be stuck in marital quicksand, relating to each other in unhealthy patterns that felt nearly impossible to escape. And, in fact, those times *were* impossible to escape… on our own. But by God's grace and mercy, he pulled us out of each pit, restored our relationship, and put a deeper affection for one another into our hearts. God not only restored us over the course of years but helped us to thrive, both individually and as a couple.

When Jeff and I got married, we had both already come to faith in Jesus. We knew we wanted our faith in Christ to be central in our marriage—we just had no clue what that meant or how it would play out! But God alone has been faithful and has always shown up for us as individuals and in our relationship with each other.

The Gospel brought healing to us individually and to our marriage before we ever heard of the Enneagram. And yet, the Enneagram has been an amazing resource and tool to illuminate our hearts to see if they're aligned with the Gospel, misaligned to some degree, or out of alignment entirely. It has helped us to see where we are misunderstanding each other and then use that insight to both turn toward God, and help us turn toward each other, in a more God-honoring way. Using the Enneagram from this biblical perspective was a significant turning point for us and our marriage.

The Enneagram became a tool for our growth and sanctification in Christ. Though it's a great tool by itself, it's an exponentially more powerful tool in the hands of God shaping us than it is in our hands alone.

But if you hear nothing else, please hear this:

The Enneagram is an insightful tool,
*but the **Gospel** is the transformation.*

As Jeff and I began talking about sharing our story and how God has used the Enneagram in our relationship, we decided we first needed to start by sharing what we believe to be true theologically (after all, Jeff is a pastor!).

So, before we go any further, it's important for us to share with you what we believe… because faith truly is what sustains and encourages us individually and as a couple.

We'll begin by saying we agree with the Gospel Coalition when they say, "The Bible is to be believed, as God's instruction, in all that it teaches; obeyed, as God's command, in all that it requires; and trusted, as God's pledge, in all that it promises. As God's people hear, believe, and do the Word, they are equipped as disciples of Christ and witnesses to the Gospel."

We believe when we place our faith in the person of Jesus Christ, three life-changing things happen:

First, we are declared ***righteous*** (Rom. 3:21–24).

Not only has Jesus Christ purchased our forgiveness for our sin, but he has also given us *his* perfect righteousness. So, the answer to the question, "Am I fully accepted by God (even with all the mess and sin in my life)?" is a resounding YES!

Second, we have been ***adopted*** (Rom. 8:14–17).

We become (never to go back to our old way of being) a beloved child of God (2 Cor. 5:17). Our adoption answers the question, "Am I loved by God?" The wonderful answer is, "YES, you are dearly wanted and cherished by God."

Lastly, we are being made *new* (Heb. 10:14).

This both *happened* to us and *is happening* to us. This means that we are changed because of what Christ has done, and at the same time we are *continuing* to change as we grow in Christ (it's a bit of a paradox!).

It's truly the answer to the question, "Is it *really* possible to change?" The most amazing and comforting answer is "YES!" We are always in the process of changing by working with the Holy Spirit to become more like Christ, who loved us and gave himself up for us.

That is the Gospel; the Good News!

And that's why we hope you will come to a deeper and richer understanding of "who you are and Whose you are."

When we know "who we are," our heart's motives and needs, we are able to see God's grace and love for us in making payment for our sins through Christ's finished work on the cross.

And when we think of "Whose we are," we now know that we are his most cherished and beloved child who he sustains and loves because of Christ's sacrifice on our behalf.

Because of God's character, his love never changes, and it doesn't depend on us "getting better" or "doing better." He simply loves us and desires for us to be in a relationship with him. We become more like him by surrendering and depending on the Holy Spirit to transform us.

Which leads us back to look at who we are. The Lord tells us he cares about our heart's motives ("For the Lord sees not as man sees:

man looks on the outward appearance, but the Lord looks on the heart." 1 Sam. 16:7), which means we don't just look at our external behaviors, we need to examine our interior world. For most of us, it's not rocket science to know that "the heart of our problem is the problem of our heart"!

Maybe your heart is a mystery to you. Maybe you need some help taking all of this Gospel truth and using it in a way that reveals your heart's core motivations to make a real difference in your marriage. If that's where you are, then I have some great news for you—there is help and there is hope!

The Gospel, the Enneagram, and Marriage

At the most basic level, Jeff and I know that the reason we both do all the awful stuff we do is because of sin.

From our earliest days as a married couple, Jeff and I knew we had a sin problem (and yes, it sometimes felt as if the other one of us was the one with the problem!). But we were even more frustrated because we kept habitually running into the same issues and falling back into marital quicksand.

Fortunately, we both wanted our marriage to work. We longed to understand our hearts' motives—*why we do what we do*—when we were introduced to the Enneagram.

This personality typology (*ennea* for nine; *gram* for drawing) goes beyond what we do (our behaviors) and gets at *why* we do what we do (our heart's motive). And even though there are just nine basic personality Types (or nine distinctly different ways of seeing and interacting with life), the Enneagram has multiple layers, allowing for many beautiful shades of any given personality Type.

The remarkable thing is that bringing the Gospel and the Enneagram together helps us hear the Gospel and its truths as if someone were speaking to us in our "mother tongue" (kind of like our personality Type's unique "language"), which enables us to understand it in a deeper and more transformative way.

But the foundational principle is this: *The Gospel itself is the transformation.* The Enneagram simply illuminates our heart's intent. The Enneagram can show us what's wrong; only Christ can fix it.

As you think about your Type (and your spouse's Type), we will give you some great relational tools through the lens of the Enneagram. We will teach you ways to understand yourself and your spouse and develop patience and empathy for your differences.

But the reason any of our tools and truths works is, ultimately, the Gospel.

Apart from Christ, neither Jeff nor I, or even the Enneagram, has anything to offer you. Whatever is helpful comes from the Gospel, which saved us and our marriage. And although we think it's extremely helpful, the Enneagram is just a tool that brings clarity to our inner world… while the Gospel is the transforming power of God.

Without the perfect, completed work of Christ on the cross in our lives through the Spirit, no new method of communication is going to work for long. The truth is that good relationships spring from good hearts (Luke 6:45), and only God gives us new hearts (Ezek. 36:26) when we surrender to Christ and depend solely on him to transform our hearts to be like his.

Without Jesus at the center of our hearts and in our marriages, the most we can manage is equality of resources and equality of regard. But with Jesus, each person learns to point the other person back to what is true in the Gospel.

In marriage, as in all of life, we are called to "value others above yourselves," (Phil. 2:3) and to "spur one another on toward love and good deeds" (Heb. 10:24). Our marriages should reflect Christ's sacrificial love for the church. With Jesus, each of us learns what it means to move toward our spouse with sacrificial love (the kindness and truth of Jesus in every word and action) in order for them to become fully alive in Christ (Eph. 5:21–31).

So, Jesus is not optional for your personal growth… Jesus is absolutely and utterly *vital*.

He's been vital for us and he's always come alongside us with love, mercy, and grace. The great news is that today, even though we still have our struggles, we truly *like* us.

We hope that Jesus will become the heart of your marriage. If you're curious about what a marriage can be when Jesus is at the center, read on. Because we know that with the power of the Gospel to change hearts and helpful insights from the Enneagram to change awareness and actions, your marriage can be even better than you've ever dared to dream possible.

Over time, Jeff and I have developed the ability to be open, honest, transparent, and vulnerable with our story in order to help point people back to the finished work of Christ—our real hope and rest. We desire to share our journey in becoming us because our path is a familiar one to many.

And like it was for John and Emily, *Becoming Us* is our invitation to you (and hopefully, your spouse) to join us as we share the lessons we've learned along the way and help you discover ways your marriage can be restored and even *thrive*.

So, if you're ready to do the heavy lifting in your own soul, then welcome to our beautifully well-worn kitchen table. We are with you, we hear you, and we are on your side supporting you the whole way by always pointing you to our real source of hope—Christ!

PART 1

CHAPTER 1

"Assumicide"

My friend's daughter, Stephanie, and her fiancé, Dustin, were deep in the midst of plans for their upcoming wedding one Saturday afternoon. They were running errands and making final decisions about the major details of the ceremony and reception. Needless to say, they were tired and stressed.

They were in Dustin's truck, and Stephanie looked over at him and said, "I know there are lots of details to get worked out, but one thing is really important to me. I'd like to get a nice wedding band."

Dustin looked over and said, "Why? That seems crazy."

She heard contempt in his voice. But she quietly said, "There are a lot of things that I don't care about, but I think having a nice wedding band is important."

He looked over at her and said, "Don't you think you're being a little ridiculous?"

"Well, I've always wanted a nice wedding band," she said.

Dustin said, "I just don't get it. I think it's nuts."

At this point, tears started filling in her eyes. She said, "I'm just trying to tell you this is really important to me." She got really quiet and turned her head toward the window.

Dustin could sense she was upset and said, "Look. I'm just saying I think you're being ridiculous."

Stephanie said, "If it's a matter of money, I can contribute."

"That's even more crazy," he said as his fists tightened on the wheel.

Now tears were rolling down her cheeks, and they were both tense and quiet.

She finally broke the silence and said, "It's something I'm going to have the rest of my life, and I just thought it would be good to get a nice one."

"The rest of your life? It's just one night, and I think it's a waste to spend a lot of money on a wedding band that's just for one night."

"Wait? One night? I'm talking about a wedding *band*... to go with my engagement ring, not a wedding *band* to play at the reception!"

"Really?" he said. "This whole time I thought you were talking about a wedding band to play music at the reception."

"No! I was talking about a ring!" she said as they looked at each other... and burst out laughing.

———

Sometimes we assume we know what the other person is saying when we really don't!

"Assumicide" perfectly sums up what we do in our relationships with each other. It's when we (incorrectly) believe we know another person's thoughts, feelings, and motivations. We *assume* we understand why they are behaving in a particular way, and then we respond *without asking clarifying questions*. Assumicide can lead to "killing" or damaging any relationship, but it's especially devastating in our most precious relationship—marriage.

I know I'm guilty of committing assumicide—I've made wrong and hurtful assumptions in my marriage (and with my children, my co-workers, and in just about any other relationship you can imagine!).

Committing assumicide is so easy to do because we truly believe everyone sees the world from our perspective *(which we believe is the correct perspective, right?)*. If others say or do something from a different vantage point or perspective than ours, we can feel confused and hurt, and we can end up damaging the relationship if we assume they acted with ill intent.

In fact, I remember looking at Jeff late one night (after a frustrating day when we hadn't been communicating well at all) and feeling completely baffled by this person sleeping beside me. I wished he came with an instruction manual!

Well, God, in his mercy and providence, provided just that through the insightful tool of the Enneagram.

As you read our stories and learn about the Enneagram (I'm a Type 9, known as the Peaceful Mediator, and Jeff's a Type 6, known as the Loyal Guardian), we want to invite you to think about your own story and open your heart for the Holy Spirit to bring revelation, insight, and willingness for you to allow God to come in and transform you from the inside out.

We'll start by telling you a little about us, who we are as individuals and as a couple, and we'll share some of the ups and downs in our twenty-four-year marriage—including our sometimes painful, sometimes funny, assumicide stories.

Because Jeff and I have gone to the "school of hard knocks" when it comes to committing assumicide, we would love for you to learn from our mishaps and blunders and help you avoid making some of those same devastating mistakes.

Believe me when I say we haven't graduated from the school of hard knocks, but we can say how God has redeemed us (and continues to redeem us) time and time again.

Yes, Jeff and I would say we are truly best friends. We got married when we were just twenty years old and had our two kids, Nate and Libby, by the time we were twenty-five. (It's amazing to realize how time has flown by. They're now in college!) We are blessed to be very close to our children and to have a deeply committed and loving marriage.

But before you start to commit "assumicide" and think we have this perfect marriage and family (like on social media where it looks like everyone is super happy with zero problems), we are anything but perfect!

Because we're human, we still have turbulent days and seasons, yet the insights God has given us through Scripture, pastors and counselors, good books, dear friends, and the help of the Enneagram has assisted us in being able to maintain a strong and loving marriage even when turbulence hits us.

Throughout these twenty-four years, we've had to do a lot of difficult work individually, and with each other, in order to have better communication and understanding.

In fact, it's the hardest (sometimes even painful!) work we have ever done. This process has truly exposed who we really are at our core and has driven us to fall at the foot of the cross and cling to it all the more. The paradox is that it has also become the most beautiful part, because Christ is always there to make us more like him in every way. He gives us rest, peace, and hope every time we come to him.

As you read *Becoming Us*, Jeff and I will be transparent in sharing from our personal experiences both as a couple and as individuals (since we know our examples best) and hope you will see how we became more aware of ourselves and used the truth of the Gospel to change how we relate to one another. Use our illustrations as a springboard for you to do the same for your personality Type and relationship combination.

As you read our stories and think through your own relationship dynamics, we would love for you to focus on how you are personally using the Enneagram and not just focus on, "What's it like for a Type X to be married to a Type Y?"

But as you'll find out, there is an answer to that question, and we think you'll be happily surprised at the answer!

So, as you learn about yourself and your spouse, we pray you will simply rest in Christ's finished work on the behalf of your own soul, your spouse, and your marriage. He is here with you now, so take a deep breath, rest in him, and be assured of his goodness, love, and compassion.

Because here's our goal: We want to help you strengthen your marriage while living out your truest and most authentic self in Christ. We want you not just to survive but to *thrive* in your relationship with God, each other, and yourself! So, pull up a chair to our "kitchen table," grab a cup of coffee or tea, and join us as we work together toward *Becoming Us*.

CHAPTER 2:

Our Becoming Us Story

Becoming "Beth and Jeff"

Beth

Our story of becoming us, "Beth and Jeff," started when we were freshmen in college at the University of Kansas. We met in March of 1994 and got married in May of 1995! Yep, that's quick!

Like so many couples, we were convinced we were super mature and ready to get married. We knew this because we believed we both saw the world from the *same* perspective! We had so much in common. We had the same beliefs and values, and we "knew" (assumed) we would have a happy and fulfilling marriage. Of course, we thought there might be a few bumps on the journey, but we didn't anticipate any significant problems ahead—and there was also the fact that we were in love! What could go wrong?

But if you've been married for longer than a honeymoon, you may realize that you really didn't know each other quite as well as you thought you did. In fact, if you were young like us, not only do you not know your spouse very well, you don't know yourself very well, either!

When I met Jeff, I purposely hadn't dated anyone for a while—which was a refreshing, enlightening, and inspiring time for me. Why? During that season of being alone, I discovered some unhealthy patterns in my past relationships (I now know some of it was related to me being a Type 9 and merging with other people, taking on their interests over mine). During this time of not dating, I found myself satisfied and connecting with the Lord instead of a boyfriend.

This season was sweet and life-changing. I learned that God's love and grace completely fills me so that I don't need other relationships to give me identity and fulfillment. I saw clearly that I already had what my heart longed for… Christ. This time with Christ allowed me to experience freedom from negative patterns of relating that were harmful to me and my relationships.

My first date with Jeff was a coffee date right before spring break, and thankfully he passed my very simple test—paying for my coffee and treating me with kindness and thoughtfulness! (This was an important hurdle since the last guy said to me on the same coffee date, "You can pay me back when you want." What!? Let's just say that was the last time I went out with that guy.) Jeff was kind, generous, attentive, and extremely handsome!

Jeff knew from that first date that he wanted to marry me—a fact he shared with me on our second date! Whoa! For someone who was just beginning to learn to be her own person, immediate talk of marriage scared the daylights out of me. I had to tell Jeff to back off a bit! (I should have known then that he was more decisive than I was!) But I loved the fact that he respected me, honored my boundaries, and still passionately (but appropriately) pursued me.

And the more time I spent with Jeff, the more I loved spending time with him. Our relationship grew quickly with deep and meaningful conversations. Summer came too fast, and we went our separate ways. Jeff went home to Texas, while I went to South Carolina on a college ministry project.

At the beginning of our sophomore year, when we were both just nineteen years old, we told our parents that we wanted to get married. They were understandably concerned. They asked us to wait, get to know each other better, and let them get to know us better as well so they could more fully support and guide us along the way. We agreed.

Since Jeff played football for the University of Kansas, I attended all of his football games with my parents. During that fall, my parents got to know Jeff well. They could see our love and his genuine support of me. They truly appreciated him and could see why we wanted to get married. With their blessings, Jeff and I got engaged on New Year's Eve of our sophomore year. We were so excited. We had our finances worked out and our parents' support, and we couldn't wait to get married!

But here's where the cracks started early on to reveal my own heart and internal struggles.

Not only did I have the normal load of spring semester classes, homework, and building my relationship with Jeff, I added planning a wedding with the wedding date only four months away! I began to experience a new level of anxiety and stress I'd never known before.

I didn't know it then, but my Type 9 personality was constantly urging me to merge with everyone who had an opinion about my wedding (and by "merge," I mean putting everyone else's thoughts, opinions, and desires ahead of my own). As you can imagine, accommodating everyone's desires and opinions is an impossible task! I was so overwhelmed and afraid to mess up that it affected how I thought, felt, and behaved. I was like a different person. I was irritable, scared, nervous, defensive, and controlling.

Who was this person? I didn't enjoy her, and neither did others who experienced this side of me. Jeff was very understanding and "assumed" that once we got past the wedding, I would go back to my peaceful and fun-loving self.

At the end of those four (beyond stressful) months, Jeff and I finally got married!

So here we were, two newly married people who didn't know really much of anything about each other or ourselves, trying to do a new dance together.

We assumed while we were dating that, since our relationship was like amazing professional ballroom dancers, we'd become the most amazing marriage partners. Our dating life had been so rich, deep, and meaningful that we truly thought we knew what we were in for—we were going to continue in our marriage in the same way as our dating experience and be a couple with almost no problems.

Instead, we found ourselves stepping on each other's toes and falling over each other time and time again. It just didn't make sense; we couldn't understand why this was happening. But we quickly realized we didn't know each other, or ourselves, very well at all. Not only were we not professional ballroom dancers, we didn't even know how to slow dance! (Maybe you can relate to this struggle.)

I truly believe that if we'd had the tool of the Enneagram from a Gospel perspective, it would have helped us to avoid this kind of friction and allowed us to approach each other with more kindness and understanding.

But God had other plans and ways for us to learn these things and eventually pass them along to you. But what we learned that changed the course of our relationship actually needed to start by looking back in time to us growing up as two vastly different human beings and the impact that was having on our relationship.

Becoming Beth

By God's grace, even though I had a significant reading disability growing up, I had a great family who loved me and encouraged me.

My dad, a Type 7 (the Entertaining Optimist) is a physician, while my mom, a Type 6 (the Loyal Guardian) is a nurse; she stayed home with my brother and me until we entered middle school. My childhood, with a few exceptions, was pretty peaceful and so positive that I still have a great relationship with both my parents. My dad's super-optimistic and encouraging personality allowed me to feel very affirmed growing up, which helped me thrive as a child. My mom's loyal, faithful, hardworking personality taught me the importance of being responsible and thoughtful of others.

Not long into my study of the Enneagram, I resonated with the Type 9 (the Peaceful Mediator). As I reflected on my childhood and teen years, I could see how that Type made sense with my life story.

My brother, Mark, who is four years older, loved to torment me (like all siblings do) when we were kids. In the early 1980s, my parents bought one of the first television sets with a remote control (I know I'm dating myself here!). When you pushed a button, a red light would appear on the remote. Mark convinced me that it was a laser, and if he aimed it at me, it would hurt me. Whenever he wanted to have fun at my expense, all he had to do was aim that remote in my direction and I would run for my life throughout the house with him close behind... of course, with him laughing at me the whole way.

Now that we're adults, I have to admit it's kind of funny that he chased me around with the remote, but don't tell him that! In case you're wondering, my adult relationship with my brother is great.

He's a Type 2 (the Supportive Advisor) and is a seminary professor and amazing husband, father, and friend—and it helps that he no longer chases me around with the laser remote!

But when we were kids, Mark also found it hilarious to sit on top of me so I couldn't move, the way big brothers often do! He didn't do anything to me except laugh while keeping me from getting away. I, of course, tried everything in my power to get free. But his laughter and teasing would hit a "nuclear" button inside me, and I'd become enraged.

I'd transform from being the peaceful and kind Dr. Banner, from the Marvel comic books, into being the raging Incredible Hulk (or at least it felt that way). But truthfully, my Incredible Hulk wasn't powerful at all, except within myself. I hated it when this furious part of me showed up, because it felt too big and powerful. I simply wanted to be at peace and in harmony—especially with Mark.

This kind of internal eruption—from peaceful to enraged—followed me into my adult years, even though it only revealed itself occasionally since I was constantly pushing it down to suppress it. Only recently have I realized that it can actually have a positive purpose (though it's still uncomfortable), and I've had to do a lot of internal self-awareness to work on it and use it correctly to express and assert myself.

When I entered kindergarten, I was a happy, bold, and confident little girl, well liked and athletic, a great peacemaker who made friends with girls and boys equally. This personality trait remained throughout life. But in first grade I hit some major speed bumps—I had a very hard time learning to read (I later got diagnosed with a reading disability that ran in the family). Before I got the right help, I felt stupid and inadequate, causing great amounts of shame to follow me throughout elementary school and into adulthood. Shame made me believe the lie that I didn't matter, even though my parents did a wonderful job saying otherwise.

I knew along with my parents' love, I had the love of God. Even as a young child, I always had a faith that God existed and somehow wanted a relationship with me. In fact, there was a spiritual awareness happening in my whole family that changed our hearts and our relationships as we embraced the Gospel in the early 1980's.

However, all that love and the truth of the Gospel didn't erase the fact that I was hard-wired with a Type 9's tendencies toward not wanting conflict, which became more apparent as I grew older.

In high school I began dating and found myself merging with my boyfriend. (I didn't know what I was doing at the time but, looking back, merging was exactly what I was doing—always putting his wants and desires before my own.)

Believing that "just being me" was never going to be good enough, I was desperate to find out what made him happy. I believed I had to invest fully in who I was dating, but in doing that, I lost "me." Somehow, being lost felt more comfortable than asserting myself— even though it could have had awful consequences. I was just going along to get along.

When it was time to go to college, I didn't have any major ambitions, hopes, or dreams. I was on "cruise control," just doing whatever was necessary to keep the peace and remain comfortable (that's a very Type 9 thing!). I only applied to one college, the University of Kansas, because it was close, familiar, and convenient. I was a fourth-generation Jayhawk, and KU seemed like a good and easy fit.

As I have come to understand myself, Type 9s are often walking around in an internal fog. Knowing ourselves (our passions, desires, abilities, and opinions) is hard for us; I didn't know "what I wanted to be when I grew up" so I opted for general studies my freshman year. When I later discovered that KU offered a degree in sign language, which I had always loved, I was able to major in sign language interpretation.

Fortunately, God had his hand on my life even when I wasn't sure what direction I was heading. I found a Christian community with Cru, a collegiate outreach ministry at KU. I started dating a guy, but it didn't last very long. Afterward, I began my season of seeking to know God and have him fill the hole in my heart. During this life-transforming time for me, I was immersed in a community that focused on God's love and how he alone fills me with the message my heart longs to hear. And then, in God's sweet mercy, I met Jeff, who had been on his own journey with God and family.

Becoming Jeff

Jeff

I grew up as an only child "deep in the heart of Texas," the adopted son of a commercial electrician and a homemaker. My mom, a Type 2 (the Supportive Advisor) stayed home and cared for me along with other children from our extended family. She had major health issues and was unable to have her own biological children, which is why God placed me in her life and my dad's. My mom's chronic illness meant that in different seasons of my childhood she was often either in the hospital or recovering from being in the hospital, and we never quite knew how she was doing.

My dad, a Type 9 (the Peaceful Mediator), has always been a steady presence in my life, particularly in light of my mom's poor health. He often took me hunting and fishing and coached me in soccer and baseball. When I began playing football, he'd often help out as I was practicing place kicking. I always knew he loved me and my mom. (Some of my fondest memories of my father are of him serving and gently caring for my mom when she was sick.)

In the midst of the difficulties of my mom's illness, as well as some of the impacts of adoption, I became a strong-willed kid with big emotions. I was also a big kid, physically, too! Left on my own a lot, I pretty much did whatever I wanted, whenever I wanted, doing things that no child that age should be doing. At times it was fun, but other times I would find myself in difficult situations, not knowing which way to turn. When things seemed out of control, I felt sadness, anger, and hopelessness to change. I didn't know why I did what I did, but I knew deep down that I was making some poor decisions.

My freshman year of high school was an exciting time, and I loved being involved in all sorts of sports, although I made the decision to step away from football and baseball to focus on soccer. Yet, one day while heading out to soccer practice with a soccer ball at my feet, I decided to take a shot on the goal from the fifty-yard line of the football field. My shot went over the goal, which was under the football uprights. I had just hit a sixty-yard field goal with a soccer ball. I guess I shouldn't have been surprised that a football coach took notice!

The following day, the football coach invited me to try out for the freshman place kicker position. I went out on a Tuesday to my first practice, and on Thursday I played in my first game. Two games later I made a fifty-yard field goal! (It was a pretty awesome thing for a freshman!)

But football wasn't just about athletic accomplishment. When I look back on that time, I believe God used football in my life as a tool to show me his kindness and his love.

He sent me coaches and mentors, men who showed me true generosity and guided me when I was going astray. One of my coaches directed me to the guidance counselor when I didn't know how to begin the process of applying to college. And another coach, Coach Norris, literally saved my life by setting my feet on the only sure path to life: the Gospel.

One day Coach Norris pulled me aside and asked me, "Jeff, do you know why you're such a good football player?"

"Shoot, yes," I answered. "I work my tail off."

He smiled. "That's true, but the reason you're good in the first place is because your ability is a gift from God."

That first mention of God stayed with me, though I didn't act on it at the time. I went through high school still willful, going down a path that could have ended very badly for me.

Then (in God's mercy!) I set my sights on a girl who was a Christian. I came up with a very creative plan to ask her out on a date by attending her church one Sunday morning.

My "in" was through the Henry family, who were close friends. I had played soccer with their son since I was three. Their family knew the struggles I had at home, and they had been very kind to me throughout the years. They always gave me an open invitation to attend church and youth activities with them at Mimosa Lane Baptist Church and I went with them on occasion through the years.

Despite their being gracious and welcoming, I wasn't crazy about church. But as it turned out, the girl I wanted to date happened to attend the Henry's church. So, I decided to go to a service where I knew she'd be.

(Let's be clear: I wasn't going to get involved in the actual church. I was just waiting for my chance to get a date!)

What happened next was nothing I can fully explain.

Throughout the service, I found my heart being pulled toward God as I heard the message that he loved me and had paid the price for my sins. I was overwhelmed by his love for me.

That morning I began a relationship with Jesus and my life was forever changed.

Being young and new to the faith, I initially thought God would want me to "work" for him to earn grace. But through his mercy, I learned he wanted me to love him, know him, and let him change my heart and my life.

From that point on, I made it my life's purpose to share Christ's love with others.

At the time, I was still playing football and was actually being recruited to play Division I college football. When the time came to choose a college, I chose the University of Kansas for two reasons.

First, I felt loyalty to them as they were the earliest school to offer me a football scholarship. Second, on my campus visit I found a church near the school that I liked, Grace Evangelical Presbyterian Church. Once I got involved in church, finding the right church home was definitely a priority for me.

I know without a doubt that, despite my decision not to play for a more successful Division I program, I made the right decision. Because Beth was waiting for me at KU.

And one night in March my freshman year, I asked her out for coffee…

Married Life Is Hard Work!

Beth

Marrying Jeff fourteen months after we met during the spring of our freshman year meant that I started my junior year in college as a new bride. I believed that this year would be the beginning of a sweet, fun, and easy season. But I soon discovered that married life was anything but easy!

When you blend two people with sin natures from different backgrounds, family dynamics, interests, and personalities, you are inevitably going to experience some bumpy times, if not outright *extreme* turbulence.

I quickly realized that the stress I was experiencing before our marriage had followed me into marriage, where I was carrying a full load of classes, working part-time, caring for my husband, and trying to do it all flawlessly. I was petrified of not making others happy—especially Jeff. I was committing "assumicide" *all the time*. I would assume what others wanted and then I would jump through any hoop to come through for them.

But there was a huge flaw: I would be greatly disappointed when either I couldn't come through as well as I thought I should, or they didn't seem as happy or as satisfied as I had hoped.

Sadly, I continued this pattern for *years,* and it only brought despair, resentment, loneliness, and a false view of what was happening in life. I was convinced that what I assumed was true and real, and I continued to spiral downward. Instead of realizing that I might be seeing and interpreting others and life incorrectly, I started to blame others that I couldn't be happy and content.

This desperation to make others happy, especially Jeff, was all consuming. My personality clung like a magnet to his likes, his desires, and his calling. I no longer put my focus equally on myself and Jeff; I almost solely focused on him.

I was confused. As a "good Christian wife," wasn't I supposed to make him happy? Wasn't I supposed to lose myself and become "one" with him?

I discovered the answer was both yes and no. Yes, it was good to want to make him happy and become "one" with him in our marriage. But no, losing myself wasn't the right answer.

As I write this, my heart is saddened for that young twenty-year-old bride. I was so desperate to give myself away in order to be seen, loved, and important to my husband and others, that I didn't believe I mattered much unless I made them happy. I am saddened I couldn't see my own value and, therefore, withheld myself from truly blossoming. I am saddened that I felt losing myself in this way seemed like the right "Christian" thing to do.

That said, looking back, I can now see the beauty of God's perfect plans and timing. He revealed his truth to me over time and helped me to grow into the woman I am today; a woman who is secure in God's love and design of me and for me. I wouldn't have learned what I needed to learn without him taking me on this rugged terrain.

But at the time, I was caught in the trap of trying to make everyone happy, losing myself, and forgetting that I was loved and cherished for who I was in Christ. I would revert to the same old patterns (the struggle of a Type 9) that inevitably left me frustrated.

As you can imagine, this life of holding unreachable standards and unattainable expectations led me to being very overwhelmed and sad. When unhealthy and misaligned with the Gospel, my Type 9 personality convinced my heart of the lie that I was a horrible wife and never good enough.

These feelings directly correlated to my own unrealistic expectations of who I *assumed* I should be as a wife and Christian and not from any criticisms Jeff leveled at me. My wrong focus wasn't Jeff's doing or his desire but rather *my heart being misaligned with the truth of who I was in Christ*.

This self-judgment led me to mild depression and isolation, which added strain to our already struggling marriage.

Needless to say, we were pretty miserable.

And then we moved. (I hoped a fresh start would do the trick.)

After graduation, Jeff and I decided to join the Navigators Collegiate ministry in their two-year internship program, *EDGE Corps*.

In August 1997, we packed our car and set out for Normal, Illinois (and yes, it's pretty normal!). We moved into a basement apartment of a very sweet family. Our entire living space was less than 250 square feet. It was tight, but we made it work. We still felt like newlyweds and we were so happy to have our own space that we could call our "little home."

But if that tiny space weren't enough to create more conflict, then God had an idea to thicken the plot. Remember, not only did we still not know ourselves well, but we didn't know or understand each other, either. But in God's perfect plans he saw it good for us to add two children into the mix in the next three years.

Not surprisingly, parenthood stirred the challenging relational pot in our marriage with more tension, confusion, accusations, and weariness. We needed help and understanding. We needed to figure out why we continued to get stuck day after day in the same old patterns of relating—patterns that weren't working. But it felt that no help was in sight.

Jeff (as a Type 6) was always on the lookout for problems and continued to take care of himself, as he had done his whole life. He didn't need me to clean, cook, or serve him in any of the ways I assumed he needed from a wife.

One day, in exasperation, I finally said, "Jeff, I don't know how to love you!"

He didn't know what to say. He was trying everything he knew to encourage and reassure me, but he didn't understand me. We were missing each other. Our off-kilter efforts toward each other landed on wounded hearts.

Despair and loneliness crept in as we tried to hang on the best we knew how.

And then we moved, again.

CHAPTER 3:

Discovering the Enneagram

Our Need

Jeff

After Nate was born in 1998, Beth and I packed up our growing family, left Normal, and headed to Covenant Theological Seminary in St. Louis. We were living the "seminary lifestyle," which basically meant we were poor as church mice. We were also going there to lead a campus ministry at St. Louis University. I was a full-time grad student, part-time collegiate ministry worker, a full-time husband, and a young dad. It was a stressful and demanding season, to say the least!

During this time, I felt exposed and ill-equipped, not understanding even where to begin, given the responsibility to love my wife of four years, my one-year-old son, and the new baby that Beth was carrying at the time. We lived in an apartment complex on

25

the seminary campus, along with all the other sacrificing students and their families.

Yet, one particular moment during these stressful seminary days brought radical Gospel transformation into my life.

Our dumpster was on the far side of the parking lot from where we lived. After yet another argument with Beth, I left for work feeling the heavy baggage of my heart. As I walked out of our apartment, I grabbed the trash and put it in the car to drive to the dumpster.

Driving that short distance through the parking lot, I heard the hymn "Jesus I Come" on the radio for the first time. My heart was captivated so fully that I had to pull over and stop the car. There I was sitting in the parking lot, listening to this song, and weeping.

With tears streaming down my face, I heard these words being sung over me: "Out of my bondage, sorrow, and night, Jesus, I come; Jesus, I come. / Out of my shameful failure and loss, Jesus, I come; Jesus, I come. / And out of my sin and into thyself, Jesus, I come to thee."

In this one moment in time, God captured my heart with the truth of the Gospel in an experiential way; a new way. And I thought to myself, if these words could be true for the writer of this song, maybe they could be true for me.

Right then, I chose to trust the Gospel and believe it in every part of my life.

As a start, I began to trust the Gospel by apologizing to Beth. My plan was very simple. If she said that I hurt her feelings, misspoke to her, or criticized her, all she needed to do was say, "Jeff, what you did was hurtful." And I would apologize, without justification and without defensiveness.

I was able to do this because I finally understood that I *am* safe and secure in the finished work of Christ on my behalf. I now understood that not only were all my sins forgiven and cast away from God, but that Christ's perfect righteousness was securely placed on me. This meant I could (finally) completely rest in the security I had in Christ. I knew where my true identity was now, no matter how hard our relationship seemed.

It took Beth several weeks to begin to trust this change in me; she needed to see the reality that what was happening was true in my heart. For me, part of the change was beginning to realize that I was often unaware of how my actions and behaviors impacted my wife. I wanted to trust Beth to speak into my life for my good and for the good of my relationship with Christ.

But I didn't turn into a "saint." Even though I knew God was working in my heart and in our marriage, I was at my wit's end because of the old patterns and ruts that we were in.

Our arguments were unproductive, and I didn't know how to change them. Our communication wasn't effective, and we were both frustrated. Even though we both felt loved by our parents, we had inherited from our families very different ways of coping with problems. Yes, we had a vision for the other person's life, but it was the vision of our idea of what we wanted *them* to become.

Sadly, we didn't know it, but we wanted to change each other so we would feel better about ourselves. The way we tried to accomplish this was to criticize and "bark" at each other (or retreat) until we broke down and finally changed. Obviously, this strategy wasn't effective or helpful, but it was our default pattern. And it wasn't working for either of us!

As I think about it now, Beth and I were just twenty years old when we got married, and we were basically still "kids." We had a lot of maturing to do. It wasn't until a few years into our marriage that I began to recognize how ill-prepared I was for the dynamics I was facing in both marriage and parenthood.

Deep down I knew if we were going to do marriage well, we'd have to be able to know our hearts on a deeper level and be able to communicate at this level with our spouse.

I also knew we often unfairly expect our spouse to fulfill our deepest needs, though God never designed or intended them to fulfill us perfectly. In fact, it's impossible for them to do so. How are they supposed to be able to fulfill these needs when most of the time we can't fully name what our deepest needs and longings are for ourselves?

The only one who can fully fulfill our needs is Jesus Christ. To expect our spouse to do what only Jesus can do is incredibly unfair and unkind.

As believers, Beth and I were committed to Christ and each other, but practically speaking, we were pretty naïve and frustrated. We were young with a young family, and we didn't know what we were doing. In fact, we didn't even know where to start to find out what we needed to learn.

We needed help. We were completely stuck in our patterns of relating and sinking more and more into the pit of despair. How could we understand one another? How could we offer our love to the other so that they actually received it and felt it deeply? We needed an instruction manual that was much more specific to us, how we saw the world, and how we related to one another.

Encountering the Enneagram

Beth

It was around 2000, and our little family was squished into a tiny seminary apartment. Jeff was learning lots about theology and discovering what it meant to love Christ with both his head and his heart. He would often share that he identified so much with the apostle Paul when he said, "I do not understand my own actions. For I do not do what I want, but I do the very thing I hate" (Rom. 7:15).

I knew what he meant. He was struggling because he wanted to be Christlike, but when we would get into conflict, he wouldn't respond the way he wanted to. The same was true for me.

I understood.

I knew the Gospel. I knew that Christ loved me and had died for me, bringing me freedom and fullness in him. But somehow, I was struggling to let that truth settle fully into my heart and life. I kept falling into the *same* ruts over and over, and I felt stuck. This failure to grow caused me great guilt, shame, and fear. I couldn't seem to grasp the freedom I knew I already had. I was scared, lost, lonely, and very reactive with my family.

Thankfully, Jeff and I had dear friends, Travis and Susan, who had been in the same boat as us. When they saw how we were struggling (it wasn't something we tried to hide; we were frustrated and desperately wanted help), they gave us a key that would end up unlocking hope and change in our marriage.

Travis and Susan came over for dinner one night and brought a book they thought might be helpful for us to understand not only *why* we do what we do, but also how we could apply grace and forgiveness to all of life. It was Richard Rohr's book *The Enneagram: A Christian Perspective.*

Jeff skimmed through the Enneagram book… and I *devoured* it.

I dove in because it offered something I was desperately seeking from the Lord: clarity for my internal world. You see, when I read about the Enneagram, I resonated with the Type 9, and in an almost humorous way, I discovered that 9s know ourselves the least! But I finally had a book in my hand that cleared away the fog, illuminated my internal world, and brought a sense of understanding to what was going on inside me. It revealed to me what I could never have understood about myself on my own.

Not only did the Enneagram help me see my own life clearly, but I began to see Jeff through a different lens, too. Seeing him differently helped me to know him on a much deeper level. It allowed me to have more compassion, kindness, forgiveness, mercy, and grace for Jeff (and ultimately for myself).

As I began to understand the Enneagram, I often said to myself, "Oh, that's why I do that!" And equally as often I'd think, "Oh, that's why he does that!"

Everything was making sense, which allowed my restless heart to find much needed rest. As I leaned into Jesus, with the help of the Enneagram, Jeff and I actually began to work together to change our relationship in a deep and lasting way.

During these early years of learning about the Enneagram, I was beginning to see why I struggled internally in my marriage and in my life as a whole. But the Enneagram not only revealed why I struggled, it also revealed to me my own path of growth—and learning how to grow was exciting!

The Enneagram was quickly becoming a powerful tool to help me navigate my internal world as well as improve my relationship with my husband.

Here's what I began to learn…

CHAPTER 4:

The Enneagram

It's All About the WHY

Beth

While personality tests are fun and informative, and offer some value, most of them focus on external behaviors. Where they fall short is that they don't give you the tools to transform yourself from the inside out to become the friend, spouse, and follower of Christ you long to be.

However, the Enneagram works differently. Again, it reveals not *what* we do, but *why* we do it. From the Greek words for nine (*ennea*) and drawing (*gram*), the Enneagram is a nine-pointed geometric symbol. Each point represents a basic personality Type and a specific pattern of thinking and way of being. This means there are nine valid perspectives of the world. You can think of it like wearing different colored lenses—if you have red lenses, you see the world in red, but if you have green lenses, you see the world in green. The same goes for orange, blue, yellow, etc. It's hard to remember that other people aren't seeing the world through the same colored lens that you are!

At first glance, the Enneagram symbol you see in most places can be looked at with confusion and some have mistakenly viewed it as an anti-Christian symbol, which it is not. But to be clear, we have taken the typical Enneagram symbol and made our logo more graphically representative of what we believe: nine different colored dots to remind us that everyone is different! We are hoping when you see these nine different colored dots that you will remember they represent *people*, the body of Christ. These dots represent us, the church. We are all different, yet we are all uniquely who God made us to be. When we unify in our diversity, we glorify God and bless others.

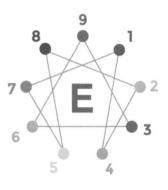

That's why our purpose for studying the Enneagram is to learn why each Type thinks, feels, and acts in specific ways. With this information, coupled with our assurance in Christ, we can look at ourselves honestly, then surrender and depend on Christ to renew us into his likeness.

What a powerful resource! It has the potential to impact every relationship in our lives. It can positively transform our relationships with ourselves, others, and most importantly with God. But before going any further, I want to reiterate how important it is to use the Enneagram correctly.

The Enneagram is the most exposing and revealing personality typology we have encountered because it's *not* just trying to explain what we do on the outside. Instead, it's telling us *why* we think, feel, and behave on the inside. It clearly reveals to us our Core Motivations as well as the condition of our heart. It will tear down any facade we try to hide behind.

However, because the Enneagram so deeply exposes why we think, feel, and behave in particular ways, if used incorrectly, it can cause great harm to others and ourselves. Please, never use the Enneagram as a sword causing harm to another person through mocking, teasing, or belittling them for their Type. This will never bring about the unity and beauty that God calls us to experience in our relationships together.

Equally as important, we should never use the Enneagram as a personal shield—where we hide behind our personality traits through defending, fighting, ignoring, or blame shifting.

Instead, it's essential that we see, own, and ask for forgiveness for our weaknesses and sins. We can be vulnerable in this way because we know everything has been completely taken care of in Christ's finished work on our behalf and his righteousness placed on us. We no longer have to live as slaves to fear, self-condemnation, or shame, for Christ has set us free from bondage and adopted us as his beloved children (Eph. 1:5).

When we use the Enneagram from a biblical perspective, the tender mercy of the Holy Spirit opens our minds and hearts to a new way of living in the freedom and grace that are ours in Christ. He calls us to understand one another at a deep level, just as he knows each of us and loves us. Knowing one another allows us to know how to build one another up uniquely, according to our Types, while also bringing the work of reconciliation to all. God created us uniquely different so we can come together and bring him glory, honor, and praise.

The Enneagram as a GPS

As you travel together on this road trip called marriage, the Enneagram is like an internal GPS (like the kind we use in our car for navigation) that helps you to understand why you and others think, feel, and behave in particular ways.

This internal GPS assists you in knowing your current location (your main Enneagram Type) and your Type's healthiest destination, living in alignment with the Gospel.

In a similar way, the Enneagram can also act like a rumble strip on the highway. The rumble strip is that boundary on the road that makes an irritating sound warning you when you're about to go off course, swerve off the road and land in a ditch, or worse, hit oncoming traffic, hurting yourself or others.

The Enneagram is simply a tool, like a GPS, to help you know where you are, where you are currently heading (whether on your best path or veering off course), and where your healthiest destination is in Christ.

It brings astonishing clarity to why you do what you do, *but the Enneagram itself cannot transform you.* It is only a tool and resource. The Gospel is the only thing that can bring real and lasting transformation to your life (Rom. 1:16–17). Only the finished work of Christ has the power to change you and free you to be the best version of who he created you to be.

And notice what I said: you have the Enneagram to guide *you*, not to help you guide, fix, or change your spouse. (Tempting as it is!)

The work you are doing is internal work to change you. The Enneagram has great rewards and benefits. But the work you do is your own work through the power and guidance of the Holy Spirit. However, if you change your own habits of relating and ways of perceiving, your marriage will change, *even if your spouse doesn't use the Enneagram.*

If you're ready to do this revealing, internal work, you'll need to start by figuring out your Type. And while it's true that everyone uses all the nine Types to varying degrees, we call just one Type our "Main Type."

Remember, the Enneagram will reflect to us the current condition of our hearts and help us know when our hearts are drifting away from the Gospel. This awareness allows us to wake up, confess, and ask the Holy Spirit to return our hearts to our best path in becoming more like Christ.

Before trying to find your Type, please remember that although the Enneagram may seem simple, it is really rather complex. That's why it's good to learn about each of the Types and give yourself time to figure out what Type best fits you. Don't be discouraged if it takes you a long time to discover your true main Type. (It actually took Jeff almost five years to figure out his Type and another year to accept it, so taking time to figure out your Type is nothing to be ashamed of!)

In fact, if you're not sure right away, it's okay to narrow your Type down from nine Types to two or three Types. "Try on" one of the Types for a while to see if the underlining motivations are the core reasons you think, feel, and behave the way you do. Then try on a different number that seems like you and do the same thing. Continue this pattern until you truly can see *why* you think, feel, and behave from your core in one particular Type.

Also, be aware that when you do find your Type, you may feel somewhat uncomfortable and exposed. It's natural for people not to want to be their main Type! We are being fully exposed to all aspects of our inner being, and many of the things we have kept hidden will now have a spotlight on them. That exposure can cause shame, fear, and self-condemnation.

But if these feelings arise, please take a big, deep breath, turn to God, and repeat what Jack Miller always said: "Cheer up! You're a worse sinner than you ever dared imagine, and you're more loved than you ever dared hope."

Jeff and I love that quote because it reminds us that we are totally free in Christ, who loves us as his cherished and beloved children. His love will allow you to accept (and even embrace) your Type while also asking God to enable you to move toward the healthier aspects of your Type so you are more aligned in Christ.

We all have the ability to change and grow.

But first, in order for you to truly discover the Type that fits you best, you need to look at your Core Motivations.

Getting to the Core

It's important to understand that although we access all nine Types to varying degrees, only *one* main Type drives our personality.

Your Type has many important factors, but there are four "Core Motivations" that are the driving force behind your thoughts, feelings, and actions: Core Fear, Core Desire, Core Weakness, and Core Longing.

We use the nine personality strategies (1–perfectionism, 2–helping, 3–achieving, 4–creating, 5–thinking, 6–preparing, 7–planning, 8–protecting, or 9–withdrawing) to protect ourselves from our Core Fear and Core Weakness and to get our Core Desire and Core Longing met.

But please understand this: The Enneagram is like a nonjudgmental friend who names and addresses the core dynamics of your heart. It invites you on to a path of discovery and growth. By learning the nine different colored lenses (perspectives), you will discover your Core Fear, Core Desire, Core Weakness, and Core Longing. As a bonus, you'll also grow in understanding, empathy, compassion, grace, mercy and, hopefully, forgiveness in your relationships with yourself, your spouse, family, and others.

Using the Enneagram from a Gospel-centered approach will enable you to see how the finished work of Christ has *already satisfied* your Core Longing and has completely taken care of your Core Fear, Core Desire, and Core Weakness in a way that benefits you and glorifies him.

The four Core Motivations are:

1. **Core Fear**—What you're always running away from, avoiding, and trying to prevent from happening.

2. **Core Desire**—What you're always striving for and believing will bring you complete fulfillment in life.

3. **Core Weakness**—The core issue you're always wrestling with, which will remain a struggle until you're in heaven, like the "thorn in my flesh" Paul described in his own life in 2 Corinthians 12:7–10: "A thorn was given me in the flesh, a messenger of Satan to harass me, to keep me from becoming conceited. Three times I pleaded with the Lord about this, that it should leave me. But he said to me, 'My grace is sufficient for you, for my power is made perfect in weakness.' Therefore I will boast all the more gladly of my weaknesses, so that the power of Christ may rest upon me… For when I am weak, then I am strong."

   Therefore, you must surrender yourself to Christ and depend on him solely to transform your heart to be more like his. The more you are surrendering, depending, and resting in your true identity in Christ, the weaker the grip the Core Weakness has on you. But your Core Weakness will continually pop up throughout life and create problems for you.

4. **Core Longing**—The central message that your heart is always longing and thirsting to hear. Jeremiah 2:13 says, "My people have committed two sins: They have forsaken me, the spring of living water, and have dug their own cisterns, broken cisterns that cannot hold water."

This reveals why you're thirsty and how you're intentionally seeking to satisfy that thirst on your own. But the good news of the Gospel is that Christ's life, death, and resurrection completely satisfy this Core Longing, allowing your heart to rest fully in the fact that Christ tells you this. When you're trying to fill yourself with this message apart from him, you will always thirst for more. But when you listen and see that he is directing you to him, the Spring of Living Water, to drink and have your fill, you'll then find that you are already completely fulfilled and set free. The beautiful part of the Gospel is that, though you've sought this from people your whole life and they have fallen short in providing this message to your heart's content, the finished work of Christ (the Gospel) offers it to you completely. Jesus fully satisfies your heart's Core Longing, which completely frees you and allows you to rest fully in the truth of the Gospel.

The Nine Types and Their Core Motivations

Type 1:

- **Core Fear:** Being wrong, bad, evil, inappropriate, unredeemable, or corruptible.
- **Core Desire:** Having integrity, being good, balanced, accurate, virtuous, and right.
- **Core Weakness:** *Resentment*—Repressing anger that leads to continual frustration and dissatisfaction with yourself, others, and the world for not being perfect.
- **Core Longing:** "You are good."

Type 2:

- **Core Fear:** Being rejected and unwanted, being thought worthless, needy, inconsequential, dispensable, or unworthy of love.
- **Core Desire:** Being appreciated, loved, and wanted.

- **Core Weakness:** *Pride*—Denying your own needs and emotions while using your strong intuition to discover and focus on the emotions and needs of others, confidently inserting your helpful support in hopes that others will say how grateful they are for your thoughtful care.
- **Core Longing:** "You are wanted and loved."

Type 3:
- **Core Fear:** Being exposed as or thought incompetent, inefficient, or worthless; failing to be or appear successful.
- **Core Desire:** Having high status and respect, being admired, successful, and valuable.
- **Core Weakness:** *Deceit*—Deceiving yourself into believing that you are only the image you present to others; embellishing the truth by putting on a polished persona for everyone (including yourself) to see and admire.
- **Core Longing:** "You are loved for simply being you."

Type 4:
- **Core Fear:** Being inadequate, emotionally cut off, plain, mundane, defective, flawed, or insignificant.
- **Core Desire:** Being unique, special, and authentic.
- **Core Weakness:** *Envy*—Feeling that you're tragically flawed, something foundational is missing inside you, and others possess qualities you lack.
- **Core Longing:** "You are seen and loved for exactly who you are—special and unique."

Type 5:
- **Core Fear:** Being annihilated, invaded, or not existing; being thought incapable or ignorant; having obligations placed upon you or your energy being completely depleted.
- **Core Desire:** Being capable and competent.

- **Core Weakness:** *Avarice*—Feeling that you lack inner resources and that too much interaction with others will lead to catastrophic depletion; withholding yourself from contact with the world; holding onto your resources and minimizing your needs.
- **Core Longing:** "Your needs are not a problem."

Type 6:
- **Core Fear:** Feeling fear itself, being without support, security, or guidance; being blamed, targeted, alone, or physically abandoned.
- **Core Desire:** Having security, guidance, and support.
- **Core Weakness:** *Anxiety*—Scanning the horizon of life and trying to predict and prevent negative outcomes (especially worst-case scenarios); remaining in a constant state of apprehension and worry.
- **Core Longing:** "You are safe and secure."

Type 7:
- **Core Fear:** Being deprived, trapped in emotional pain, limited, or bored; missing out on something fun.
- **Core Desire:** Being happy, fully satisfied, and content.
- **Core Weakness:** *Gluttony*—Feeling a great emptiness inside and having an insatiable desire to "fill yourself up" with experiences and stimulation in hopes of feeling completely satisfied and content.
- **Core Longing:** "You will be taken care of."

Type 8:
- **Core Fear:** Being weak, powerless, harmed, controlled, vulnerable, manipulated, and left at the mercy of injustice.
- **Core Desire:** Protecting yourself and those in your inner circle.

- **Core Weakness:** *Lust/Excess*—Constantly desiring intensity, control, and power; pushing yourself willfully on life and people in order to get what you desire.
- **Core Longing:** "You will not be betrayed."

Type 9:
- **Core Fear:** Being in conflict, tension, or discord; feeling shut out and overlooked; losing connection and relationship with others.
- **Core Desire:** Having inner stability and peace of mind.
- **Core Weakness:** *Sloth*—Remaining in an unrealistic and idealistic world in order to keep the peace, remain easy-going, and not be disturbed by your anger; falling asleep to your passions, abilities, desires, needs, and worth by merging with others to keep peace and harmony.
- **Core Longing:** "Your presence matters."

Summaries of the Nine Types

Here are summaries for each of the nine Types (you can find more details in the Enneagram Roadmap).

People use various names for each Type. One of my teachers and Enneagram expert, Katherine Fauvre, uses two-word descriptors I believe fully capture the essence of each Type. We prefer to use them, but most Enneagram teachers typically address each Type by number as the descriptive names can vary and can sometimes conjure biases, whether positive or negative.

We believe each Type reflects God's glory and creativity when we are healthy and aligned with the Gospel. We also believe each Type reflects the fall of man and our struggle with sin and death when we are not healthy or out of alignment with the Gospel. *No Type is better or worse than another.* All Types are equal; therefore, we typically refer to them by their number (or numeral).

Following the name of each Type are five descriptive words. These five words describe a Type at their best to when they are not doing well. Think of it as a spectrum from healthy to unhealthy.

To help you understand all nine, consider these summaries to see what sounds familiar or resonates with you.

Summary of Type 1: The Moral Perfectionist is conscientious, orderly, appropriate, ethical, judgmental.

You walk through life seeing the way things should be and always striving to do what is right, wanting to be responsible and improve everything around you.

However, the world is imperfect, and you can't escape feeling like these imperfections are assaulting you wherever you turn. You feel compelled to take on a personal obligation to improve these errors in the world. This overwhelming burden leaves you with chronic dissatisfaction, as the work of improving things is never finished.

You will never say you're angry because that would be "bad," and your deep desire is to be seen as "good." But you wrestle with resentment because you can't control life and make everything right.

When trying to satisfy your longing for things to be "good and right" apart from Christ, you can become perfectionistic and controlling, both of yourself and others.

Internally, you struggle to believe you are good or worthy because of the inner critic that constantly finds fault with everything you do. To silence this berating voice, you are extremely hard on yourself, striving to never make mistakes, which is exhausting.

You also struggle in relationships when others interpret your "helpful advice" as criticism and judgment or perceive you as overly demanding of perfection, even though your heart truly longs to help.

However, when your heart is aligned with the Gospel and you learn to take your longings to Christ, you are able to let go of the unrealistically high standards you hold. As you rest in Christ, you no longer have to prove you are worthy or that you need to earn the love you so desperately long to receive. Your principled and purposeful nature can then bring out the best in yourself and others, truly making the world a better place.

Summary of Type 2: The Supportive Advisor is thoughtful, generous, demonstrative, people-pleasing, possessive.

You see the world through relationships, believing all people deserve to feel that someone loves and cares for them. You take a genuine interest in others and support anyone in need through your acts of service, helpful advice, and nurturing disposition.

Because of your natural sensitivity and empathy to the needs of people who are hurting, you intuitively know how to help. You feel responsible to provide support and attend to needs whenever you encounter them. However, the immense depth of need and suffering in our world can often leave you running endlessly, with no time to take care of yourself.

Being a helper satisfies you because, deep down, you struggle to believe that the people in your life love and want you apart from the help and support you offer. In your attempt to satisfy this longing to be loved and appreciated apart from Christ, you can become people-pleasing and possessive, inserting yourself into the lives of others, ignoring boundaries, and self-centeredly finding ways to be needed.

This overwhelming burden to care for everyone else damages you when you begin to attend to others' needs without adequately dealing with your own. In your pride, you can believe you know what's best for everyone else, while being in denial about the extent of your own needs, insisting that your only concern is taking care of others.

Relationally, you can struggle when others feel crowded by your efforts to help. You may feel hurt and insecure when you aren't needed, so you try to redouble your efforts to win people over by looking for things to do and say that will make people like and depend on you.

However, when your heart is aligned with the Gospel and you learn to take your longings to Christ, you begin to take care of yourself and your own needs, knowing you are wanted and loved apart from what you can do for others. From that place flows selfless generosity and encouragement, a redemptive source of kindness and love in our world.

Summary of Type 3: The Successful Achiever is efficient, accomplished, motivating, driven, image-conscious.

You are an optimistic, accomplished, and adaptable person who is able to see all that can be achieved in life. You always excel and are able to reach ambitious goals with apparent ease and confidence.

However, in our fast-paced and comparison-driven society, there are limitless opportunities for you to achieve more, drive results, and succeed in new ways. You struggle with the belief that you must excel at everything. Burdened to appear confident, successful, and impressive, you live under constant pressure to measure your worth by external achievement and a successful image.

Your deep fear of failure, or being thought worthless or incapable, causes you to struggle with deceit, hiding parts of yourself you don't want others to see and forcing you to always portray a successful exterior. In doing so, you become unaware of who you are in your own heart, which impacts not only you, but also those in a relationship with you.

When trying to satisfy your longing for success and admiration apart from Christ, you can become excessively driven and image-conscious. Self-promotion, being competitive, and constantly comparing yourself to others, along with believing you are only as good as your last accomplishment, can lead you to burnout.

However, when your heart is aligned with the Gospel, you believe that you are loved and valued for who you really are and not for only your successes and accomplishments. Your contagious confidence, enthusiasm, and focus inspires those around you. You become a humble, inner-directed team player who champions the people around you. Using your adaptability, productiveness, and drive for excellence, you achieve incredible things for the greater good.

Summary of Type 4: The Romantic Individualist is authentic, creative, expressive, deep, temperamental.

You are a creative force with a knack for discovering beauty, originality, and value in places that others miss. Your rich interior life of thoughts and feelings creates a hunger in you for emotional intensity and authenticity. Although you see profound despair and suffering in the world, you also see joy and you bravely press into hard depths to discover meaning in all of life. You embrace a wide range of emotions and experiences, and with your knack for self-expression, you bring a unique aesthetic, depth, and creativity to any event or situation.

Just as you are eager to explore the depths of our complicated world in a search for meaning and genuine connections, you also look inside yourself to find your own unique significance and value. However, when looking into your heart, a constant feeling burdens you that you are missing something important and that you're flawed in ways no one else is. Craving ideal circumstances or love, you often cannot stop pondering what is missing in your life and exploring this sense of disconnectedness.

Struggling with feelings of envy, you compare yourself to others, longing for what you don't have and believing others have what you long to possess.

When you attempt to find your unique significance and individuality apart from Christ, you can become self-absorbed and temperamental, perpetually seeing your weakness and never your glory. Painfully self-conscious, you spend a great deal of energy ruminating in your mind on how different you are from others and navigating feelings of self-hatred, shame, emptiness, and despair. You may be anxious around others, always wondering what they think about you.

Beyond your internal strife, you can get into relational conflicts by being withholding, dramatic, and temperamental; at times you may appear self-absorbed and disinterested in others.

However, when you take the longings of your heart to Christ and step out from under the waterfall of your emotions, you bring forth your talents in ways that are truly extraordinary. You have a deep intuition for how others feel and can step into turbulent feelings with ease and compassion; they don't overwhelm you. In fact, connecting with others and their intense emotions, and being there for them in their pain, brings you great joy. With your creativity, imagination, and authentic self-expression, you are an amazing gift to the world.

Summary of Type 5: The Investigative Thinker is perceptive, insightful, intelligent, detached, isolated.

You are a perceptive, innovative observer who walks through life with curiosity, craving to learn new things. Your inquisitive mind is objective and practical, making wise decisions based on reason and knowledge.

Despite your insatiable thirst for thinking and knowing, you experience the world as an intrusive and overwhelming place. Feeling that life demands too much of you, you focus your attention on conserving your energy and resources, fearing being empty and experiencing a sense of catastrophic depletion. This intense desire to hoard and control your resources and environment challenges you and your relationships, as you can become extremely private and emotionally distant.

When you attempt to navigate life apart from Christ, your fear of being incompetent and unknowledgeable, coupled with your desire for self-sufficiency and reluctance to rely on others, can cause you to withdraw, isolate, and become emotionally distant. You often feel you must know everything before sharing your insights, and your fear of feeling incompetent overwhelms you and causes you to retreat.

This desire for knowledge, independence, and a life free from obligations can strain your relationships, which require connection, feelings, and vulnerability to be healthy. You see your spouse and their needs, but you feel ill-equipped to meet them, often perceiving them as demands. So, you distance yourself from relationships in hopes that eventually you'll feel competent enough to engage. You wonder if you'll ever be able to have enough knowledge or resources to enter the mysterious and complex world of another person.

Fortunately, when your heart is aligned with the Gospel, you discover that your needs are not a problem because Christ has fulfilled them. Then you can begin to be more generous with giving of yourself and your resources to others, moving from a fear of scarcity to a belief in abundance. You begin living not just from your head but from your heart, and the whole of who you are. That, coupled with your great vision and perspective, reflects true wisdom for the world.

Summary of Type 6: The Loyal Guardian is committed, responsible, faithful, suspicious, anxious.

You are one of the steadiest and most reliable, hardworking, and dutiful people out there. Your dependability, sense of humor, and ability to foresee problems cause you to be an incredible team player. Truly concerned about the common good, you can hold groups together.

However, below the surface, constant fear and uncertainty often plague you so that you experience the world as a dangerous place where you must be hyper-vigilant, scanning for things that could threaten your safety, security, and relationships. Whether to avoid danger or challenge it head on, you can be prone to see and assume the worst. You manage your anxiety by preemptively running through worst-case scenarios to prepare for whatever bad might possibly happen. Inside your mind is a constant refrain of, "But what about this… what about that…?"

When you forget the truth of the Gospel, you can suffer from self-doubt, worry, and catastrophic thinking, which leaves you feeling anxious and costs you your ability to relax and trust yourself and others. Your mind can become muddled, skeptical, and hesitant to make decisions. You will focus on planning for crises to give you a sense of control, safety, and security in your attempt to live in a world that is trouble-free and predictable.

In relationships, you can struggle with projecting your fears, doubts, and insecurities onto others as a means to protect yourself. The challenge is that these misplaced fears, suspicions, and doubts often erode your trust in other people, God, and yourself.

However, when your heart is aligned with the Gospel and you learn to take your fears and anxiety to Christ, you experience a transformation that brings forth great courage in your life. As you realize that you are secure in him, you begin to trust yourself more, and you experience a peace that surpasses the fears you see in the world around you. Beyond that, the world is blessed by your dedication, wit, ability to solve problems and genuine loyalty.

Summary of Type 7: The Entertaining Optimist is playful, excitable, versatile, scattered, escapist.

You are a joyful, enthusiastic, and social person who radiates optimism wherever you go. As a lover of variety, you live life "big." You're eager to enjoy all of the vast experiences this world has to offer, seeing innovation and endless possibilities everywhere.

While you bring happiness and a positive outlook wherever you go, internally you are always longing for "more" and fearful of missing out. To you, life is like cotton candy, tasting super sweet but disappearing quickly, leaving you constantly unsatisfied and wanting another bite, and then another bite. Additionally, life can be painful and hard, and it's in those places that you experience a deep, internal struggle as you attempt to avoid pain at all costs. When life gets complicated, sad, or boring, you quickly escape to things that bring you pleasure, allowing you to avoid the difficult feelings you fear.

Pursuing your need for adventure, happiness, and stimulating experiences costs you the ability to enjoy the present and find satisfaction in what you already have. You may be extremely busy, packing your schedule full of activities and adventures in order to avoid dealing with your internal anxiety, sorrow, and boredom, aiming for fun and stimulation instead. Putting painful things out of your awareness, or reframing suffering into something positive without truly dealing with it, will continue to show up in counterproductive ways throughout your life.

You can also struggle in relationships, becoming scattered, uncommitted, and unreliable. People close to you can feel frustrated if you value new experiences and things more than them. They can also feel frustrated if you are unwilling to have relational depth, which often requires dealing with challenging emotions and pain.

However, when your heart aligns with the Gospel, you become more grounded in the present moment and able to savor it with a grateful heart. Trusting that God will fulfill your internal longings, you find that your grateful, receptive, and thoughtful qualities emerge. Mixed with your natural creativity and energy to inspire others, you bring joy to the sorrows and challenges of life.

Summary of Type 8: The Protective Challenger is assertive, self-confident, intense, big-hearted, confrontational.

You engage life with a confident intensity, strength, and determination to make things happen. Your decisive and assertive leadership style causes you to be a powerful change agent in the world, especially when seeking justice and protection for people who can't advocate for themselves.

However, in our world of sin and injustice, people take advantage of others and you feel an intense need to protect yourself against betrayal and powerlessness. You maintain an invincible exterior to minimize dependency and personal exposure.

Your fear of weakness and vulnerability, joined with your thirst for control, power, and justice, can lead you to be too confrontational, domineering, insensitive, and even vengeful, apart from Christ. You attempt to provide protection for yourself by living with a thick piece of steel over your heart, since your heart is extremely tender. But don't misunderstand that strength, because behind it is fear. If other Types fear people and become passive, you fear people and become aggressive. Out of your fear of betrayal you think, "I'll control you before you can control me."

Inevitably, this self-protection ends up doing more harm than good. To protect yourself, you live in denial of any emotions that cause you to feel vulnerable, out of control, and harmed. You live as though your weaknesses never existed.

In relationships with others, you can end up sacrificing intimacy so that your vulnerability won't be discovered and used against you. However, denying yourself closeness, the giving and receiving of forgiveness, and experiencing tenderness leaves you incomplete and unable to experience the intimacy and support you were created to enjoy.

But when your heart is aligned with the Gospel and you surrender your fear of betrayal by relying on Christ, you can relinquish your need for control and allow others to see an endearing vulnerability and compassionate strength within you. From that place, you can better protect the innocent from injustice, empower others, and put your strength of leadership to use for the greater good.

Summary of Type 9: The Peaceful Mediator is thoughtful, reassuring, receptive, accommodating, resigned.

You are an easygoing, non-judgmental, patient person who longs for harmony with others and your environment. Able to see all points of view, you are a natural peacemaker and agent of reconciliation who brings a sense of calm and empathy wherever you go.

Even though you are an easygoing person, you struggle being in a world that is rife with conflict and discord, which threatens the comfort you crave. Feeling that your responsibility is to ensure people experience peace and everyone is respected and heard, you manage the stress you feel by withdrawing or numbing your feelings, dreams, and desires. You "go along to get along" to avoid the internal or external conflict you are feeling.

When trying to satisfy your longing for harmony, connection, and comfort apart from Christ, you avoid conflict and become indecisive, passive, easily overwhelmed, and numb to your life.

Internally, you struggle to believe that your voice and opinions matter; you forget and belittle yourself. Focusing too much on others, you lose your identity, merging with the thoughts, feelings, and agendas of others to achieve a false harmony. You fall asleep to yourself, yet you often feel internal frustration about being overlooked.

Your attempts for harmony eventually backfire in relationships when the people around you get frustrated by your complacency, stubbornness, emotional unavailability, and passive-aggressive responses. Your attempts to avoid conflict, ironically, create the very conflict you desperately want to avoid.

However, when your heart aligns with the Gospel, you come awake to your convictions, feelings, and passions. You believe you matter and that you make a difference in this world. You also realize that, for you, true connection comes from being willing to engage in conflict with love and courage knowing that, in Christ, peace will come. You engage more genuinely with people and your own life as you bridge differences, bring people together, and achieve true harmony for yourself and the world.

The Layers of the Enneagram

You might be wondering how there can only be nine basic Enneagram Types in the whole world when we are all so different. Well, there are nine *main* personality Types, but the many layers to the Enneagram reveal variations to each of the nine Types.

(It's similar to our understanding of colors. We know there are distinct primary colors like red, yellow and blue, etc., but anyone who has ever needed to pick out a color at the paint store knows there are infinite shades of every color!)

The real impact of the Enneagram is explaining the underlying *why* of what we do, and like primary colors, there are nine main Types.

At the center of each Type are the four Core Motivations: Core Fear, Core Desire, Core Weakness, and Core Longing. They're what drive each Type to think, feel, and behave in particular ways common to that Type.

Adding to the many layers of difference are the Levels of Alignment, which gauge how closely we're living in alignment with the Gospel. All of these nuances (features), and many more, mean that even within the same main Type, people can look *very* different.

In addition to these underlying Core Motivations and Levels of Alignment are Wings, which are the Types on either side of your main Type, and Triads, which are groupings of three Types that digest events or information from a particular Center of Intelligence: Head, Heart, or Gut Instinct.

And to help you find your way, there are lines and arrows that show you the path along the way.

If you're looking at the Enneagram Types and struggling with not being sure of your main Type, don't be discouraged. It's okay and it may just take some time for you to settle on a Type that resonates with you. It is also common for people to mistype themselves at first. Jeff thought he was a Type 8 until a counselor helped him to see he was not a Type 8 but a Type 6. It took Jeff years before he could come back to the Enneagram and say, "Okay, I think I really am a Type 6, and I'm ready to learn about myself and grow."

One other note: Once you learn about the Enneagram and become familiar with the nine Types, it's tempting to "diagnose" or "Type" other people, especially family members and close friends! But here's what is super important to remember: For the Enneagram to be most effective, a person's Type has to resonate with *their* core motivations… and we can't see that from the outside looking in.

So, while we may be able to "guess" someone's Type from the way we see them behave, we may not be accurate in our assessment because we can't *see or know* their Core Motivations. And by pointing them in a particular direction, we may inadvertently bias them toward a number that isn't quite right for them.

That's part of the reason we developed a Typing Assessment on our website, YourEnneagramCoach.com, with a free PDF download overview of all nine Types to help you (and your family and friends) find your main Type. Have fun with it! You may find it helpful in guiding you to landing on the number that most resonates with you.

Levels of Alignment with the Gospel

In 1977, Don Riso made an enormously helpful contribution when he discovered what he called the Enneagram Levels of Development (or levels of health—healthy, average, or unhealthy). We move up and down through the levels depending on our heart's condition. It is a dynamic process as we are always moving and changing.

In our work with the Enneagram from a Christian perspective, we like to refer to this dynamic as "Levels of Alignment with the Gospel."

Our inspiration for this comes from Galatians 2:14 when Paul confronts Peter with these words, "When I saw that their conduct was not in step [aligned] with the truth of the Gospel…"

If becoming like Christ is the goal of the Christian, and the Gospel is the power of God to get us there, then growth in our particular Type should be in alignment with the truth of the Gospel.

Everyone moves fluidly through the Levels of Alignment. Day to day we can move up and down throughout the levels depending on how we are doing and navigating through life.

Remember when we are knowing, believing and trusting in our identity in Christ, we are living as his beloved (healthy level). But even though we know he is good and sovereign, we can at times wander away in our mind and heart from the truth that we are his beloved and start to believe that we must take some control and live in our own strength (auto-pilot/average). And then there are times that we forget we are his beloved child completely. At this state of mind, we think we are all alone and an orphan who has to do it all on our own (unhealthy).

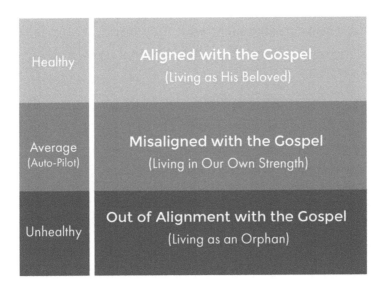

But the good news of the Gospel is that when we receive Christ as our Lord and Savior, we are always his beloved child no matter where we are on the levels of development since Christ's life, death, and resurrection accomplished everything we needed to be his. Therefore, we can look at where we really are at any given moment, rejoice at his work in our life and repent if needed, all while resting fully in who we are in him.

- When the condition of our heart is at a healthy place, we will be *aligned* with the truth of the Gospel; we know, believe, and trust in our full identity in Christ.
- When our mind and heart begin to wander from our true identity in Christ, we start to take control of our own life and become *misaligned* with the Gospel.

- And when we forget that our status is secure, we feel like an orphan and try to control all of life, living in an unhealthy manner or *out of alignment* of the Gospel.

In the Levels of Alignment with the Gospel, we are looking at just one Type at a time and seeing how that Type is doing *at any given moment*.

The Levels of Alignment with the Gospel reveal how two people of the same Enneagram Type (same Core Fear, Desire, Weakness, and Longing) can look vastly different depending on how aligned or out of alignment they are with the truth of the Gospel.

Let's take Type 8 as an example. Type 8s can be like snowplows. If you live up north or in the Midwest (as I did when I was growing up), you know that when a ton of snow is dumped on the area, the roads need massive diesel snowplows to push it out of the way so people can get to the hospital, grocery store, and other essential places.

It's not enough for everyone just to get out of their cars and start shoveling! Their efforts would simply not be enough. We absolutely need these massive snowplows to do what they were created to do and plow a path for others to move about safely. A Type 8 who is aligned with the Gospel does something similar, clearing a path for others to get where they need to go.

But a Type 8 who is misaligned with the Gospel might bump into the cars on the side of the road as they plow. When they're out of alignment with the Gospel, they will plow right over people, bringing lots of destruction and pain. Our alignment with the Gospel changes how we interact with others, God, and even ourselves.

There is some speculation that Dr. Martin Luther King, Jr. could have been a Type 8 (we obviously will never know and it's always about Core Motivations). But Dr. King seems to exemplify the beauty of a Type 8. He was willing to take on the opposition of authority on behalf of others. He was willing to protect and plow a path for others, creating a nonviolent movement that allowed others to benefit greatly for generations to come.

But a person with the same personality Type who has similar Core Motivations (Core Fear, Desire, Weakness, and Longing) can look very different when they are out of alignment with the Gospel. When out of alignment, a Type 8 can descend to plow over anyone and anything in their path.

As you can see, within the same personality Type, very different outcomes can exist, all depending on how healthy (aligned with the Gospel) or unhealthy (out of alignment with the Gospel) we are.

So, what does this development look like from a Christian's perspective?

Living as His Beloved is Alignment with the Gospel

Believers who are resting, believing, and trusting in who they are in Christ are Living as His Beloved (healthy and aligned with the Gospel). We are no longer using our personality strategies to meet our needs and desires. Instead, we are coming to our Heavenly Father, who we know loves us and will provide for us. We also know that he has already accomplished what we need and desire. As we keep our focus on him, we are filled and renewed perfectly each and every time. *This is Living as His Beloved.*

Living in Our Own Strength is Misalignment with the Gospel

When our minds and hearts wander away from fully believing and trusting in what Christ has done for us, we begin to think that we have to take care of our needs by ourselves. We are still his beloved child and know God is loving and providing, but we aren't 100 percent sure if he will do what's in our best interest. Therefore, we think we need to take over some control of our life. Getting distracted by what we want (and often demand) causes us to be misaligned with the Gospel and veer off our best path for growth. *This is Living in Our Own Strength.*

Living as an Orphan is Out of Alignment with the Gospel

When we are unhealthy or out of alignment with the Gospel, we really believe we're all alone, like an orphan. We're still God's beloved child with all the same inheritances that Christ gave us (our relationship status never changes when we are called by him), but we are now no longer experiencing this status of a beloved child. We revert to living as if we are totally on our own. Our fear and loneliness cause us to act out in ways that destroy our own lives and relationships. *This is Living as an Orphan.*

Understanding where we are in the Levels of Alignment greatly helps us to know how our heart is doing. The Levels of Alignment particular to our Type can show us when we are not fully surrendering and depending solely on the finished work of Christ. We can align with the Gospel simply by asking the Holy Spirit to take over our hearts and renew our mind.

"Do not be conformed to this world, but be transformed by the renewal of your mind, that by testing you may discern what is the will of God, what is good and acceptable and perfect" (Rom. 12:2).

The Wings

After you land on your main Type, one of the first ways each Type can vary is through the Wings. The Wings are the two numbers *directly* next to your main Type's number on the Enneagram diagram. What this means is that we access the characteristics of the Type on either side of us while remaining our main Type (with its Core Motivations).

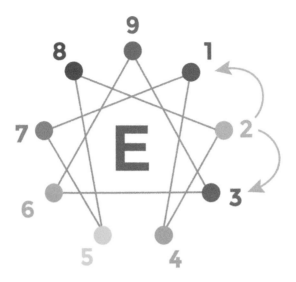

Therefore, if you are a Type 2, your Wings are 1 and 3. If you are a Type 7, your Wings are 6 and 8, etc.

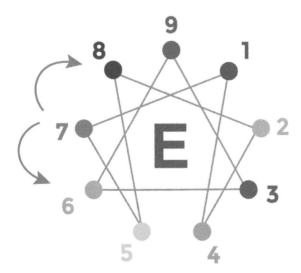

Everyone uses both Wings to varying degrees. We can also access them in different circumstances. But it's common for a person to rely more on one Wing than another. (You'll often see it written this way: 2w1 or 7w8, etc.)

Everyone is a combination of one main Type and the two Types adjacent to it.

To understand how the Wings influence your main Type, you can think of the Wings like "salt and pepper." Each Wing adds a unique "flavor" to your personality, bringing complexity to your main Type. Just like a beautiful filet mignon steak doesn't *become* the salt or pepper, neither do we become our Wings. Our Wings influence our main Type in varying ways, both positively and negatively. We know that too much salt can make that filet inedible, but the right balance can enhance our enjoyment of it significantly.

In the same way, when we are aligned with the Gospel, we can access the healthy side of the Wings on either side of our Type. But when we are misaligned with the Gospel, we will often draw from the unhealthy side of our Wings. And like under-seasoning or over-seasoning our perfectly cooked steak, it can make a huge difference.

Being more aware of how to use the "salt and pepper" of our Wings correctly can dramatically alter our experiences. When we need to get back on track to becoming aligned with the Gospel in our Type, we can choose to apply "seasoning" by utilizing the healthy attributes of our Wings.

Accessing our Wings to know, believe, and trust in our identity in Christ allows us to express ourselves more fully and to be seen for who we really are.

The Triads

We can group the nine personality Types in many ways. The most common one is by Triads, or groupings of three. These three Types share common assets and liabilities. For each person, one triad is more dominant than the other two, and that is where your main Type resides.

An emotional imbalance as well as a common desire drives each Enneagram Type in one of these three centers. Though we could name many different Triads within the Enneagram, the most well-known is the Center of Intelligence Triad:

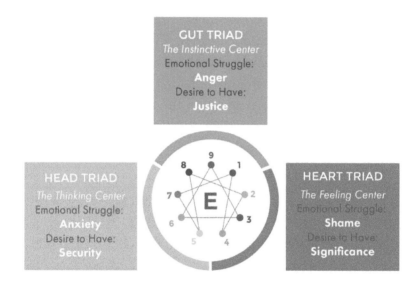

- Feeling Center (Heart Triad)
- Thinking Center (Head Triad)
- Instinctual Center (Gut Triad)

The Heart Center contains Types 2, 3, and 4, and they are *imbalanced* in their *feelings*. This group shares similar assets and liabilities surrounding their feelings as well as engaging in life and circumstances through their feelings. Type 2s feel other people's emotions. Type 3s access their emotions the least so as to not hinder them in accomplishing goals and tasks. Type 4s feel all their emotions with depth and intensity. Those in the Heart Triad share a reaction to their *emotional struggle* with *shame*.

They focus on a *common desire* for a *specific identity or significance* that they want others to see and recognize. Type 2s want to be seen as the most supportive, caring, and selfless person. Type 3s want to be seen as the most successful, admirable, and accomplished person. And Type 4s want to be seen as special, different, and unique.

The Head Center contains Types 5, 6, and 7, and they are *imbalanced* in their *thinking*. This group shares similar assets and liabilities surrounding their thinking as well as engaging in life and circumstances through mental analysis. Those in the Head Triad share a reaction to their *mental struggle* with *anxiety* (or fear). Type 5s are anxious that they do not know enough to go out into the world and do. Type 6s are anxious about all the negative possibilities that could happen in any given situation. Type 7s are anxious about being forced to focus on their inner world, trapped in emotional pain, and being deprived.

They focus on a *common desire* for *security*. Type 5s seek security through knowledge and understanding. Type 6s seek security in knowing all possibilities, having a plan for all contingencies, and having a support system in place. Type 7s seek security by avoiding the internal world of anxiety and experiencing fun, stimulation, and excitement from the external world.

The Instinctual Center contains Types 8, 9, and 1, and are *imbalanced* in their *gut instincts*. This group shares similar assets and liabilities surrounding their instincts as well as engaging in life and circumstances through their gut instincts. They share a reaction to their *instinctual struggle* with *anger*. When Type 8s see an injustice, they respond instinctually and viscerally in a fast and intense manner. Type 9s, on the other hand, are asleep to their anger because it disrupts their need for peace and harmony. They suppress their anger and are unaware that this is their instinctual struggle. Type 1s repress their anger since they believe anger is bad, but it leaks out through being critical, nit-picky, and voicing their judgments onto others.

They focus on a *common desire* for *justice*. Type 8s do not want the innocent to be harmed so they will step in and protect. Type 9s do not want others to feel overlooked or unimportant, so they will make space for others to have a voice and be heard. Type 1s do not want unethical injustices to take place so they will point out what is wrong or inaccurate so it will be addressed and fixed.

Our personality develops strategies in an attempt to compensate for our Type's imbalance. But knowing how we are imbalanced allows us to know more about our personality's structure and how to move in the direction of growth.

If you struggle with knowing your Enneagram Type, you can narrow it down by finding your Triad group first. Your main Type will be in that Triad.

The Lines and Arrows

Just like with a GPS, we need to be aware of what direction we are heading and when we need to "recalculate." The inner lines and arrows you see in the Enneagram diagram are the internal directions we take when we are in times of stress and/or in times of growth.

These directions make us aware of which direction our heart is heading and can help us determine where we end up and if we're headed off course. (But here's great news: If you find that you are headed in the wrong direction, the steps to "turning around" and getting back into alignment with the Gospel are to simply own your mistake, repent, and ask the Lord to restore you back on the path that is best for you.)

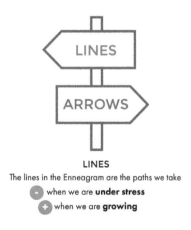

LINES

The lines in the Enneagram are the paths we take
when we are **under stress**
when we are **growing**

To use the Enneagram at a deeper level, we can access the "positive and negative" of both the Types that are connected with the lines of our main Type, as indicated by the lines and arrows.

Simply put, each Enneagram Type is connected to two other Types. It's important to realize that we always *stay in our main Type* with its Core Fear, Desire, Weakness, and Longing, but we access the attributes of the two Types our Type is connected to through the lines on the symbol. We do not become the Types we are connected to; we remain our main Type. (For more in-depth information, go to YourEnneagramCoach.com.)

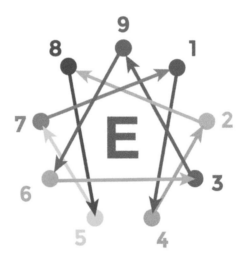

UNDER STRESS

We tend to travel down this path to the connecting Type and take on some of that Type's **average** to **unhealthy** characteristics.

In Stress—When we're under stress, we tend to take on some of the average to unhealthy characteristics of the connecting Type. It is important to see these patterns as warning signs that we are veering off course. This is our rumble strip where we need to wake up, ask for the Lord's help, and then move in the healthier direction for our personality. *(Read the Roadmap to learn more about how each Type moves in their Stress Path.)*

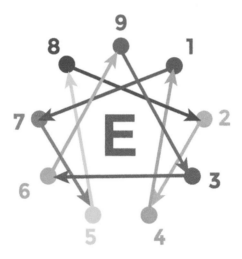

GROWTH POINT

We tend to travel down this path to the connecting
Type and take on some of that
Type's **healthy** characteristics.

In Growth—When we begin to believe, trust, and know that we are Christ's beloved child and that all he has is ours, we begin to relax and let go of our personality's constraints and lies. We begin to open ourselves to move in a healthier direction. We begin to move toward the healthier levels of the connecting Type when we are growing and aligning with Christ and how we were made. We start to feel more joy, true peace, and liberation. *(Read the Roadmap to learn more about how each Type moves in their Growth Path.)*

An Example of Stress and Growth

Beth

In showing you how these lines and arrows work, I'll use myself as an example. As you know, I'm a Type 9, the Peaceful Mediator. Type 9s don't want conflict or tension. We simply want inner stability, peace of mind, and harmony. Type 9s know themselves the least. So, it is invaluable for me to know how I might react when I am under stress as well as knowing what it looks like for me to grow.

When I am under stress, the lines and arrows show me that I will move to the average to unhealthy qualities, behaviors, and reactions of a Type 6. Under stress, I will take on the negative side of 6 and become testy, irritable, and defensive, and my mind will start racing with increased anxiety. I don't become a Type 6, but I will take on some of their attributes.

Here is an example of what stress looks like for me as a Type 9.

Last fall, Jeff and I were going to be flying to Philadelphia for an Enneagram presentation. The morning of our flight, I woke up late. This rarely happens. I scrambled to get ready and rush out the door in order to reach our flight on time. I knew that getting from Franklin, Tennessee, to the Nashville airport at 8:00 am was going to be tricky because of rush hour and slower school zones, but now we were running super late.

Even though Jeff was driving, I was irritated with every red light, every slow car, and anything that was causing more of a delay. I was thinking of all the reasons we could be slowed down even more, which would truly jeopardize our ability to catch our flight. My mind was racing, and I was a big ball of anxiety that was oozing out into the car.

As you can imagine, this reaction wasn't pleasant for Jeff to experience. But during this tense and stressful ride, I felt the Holy Spirit making me aware of a rumble strip inside me. I began to think about how I was reacting and why. I realized that I was under stress (and for good reason due to oversleeping), but my reactions were not enjoyable or helpful for those around me.

By being aware of what was going on within myself, I was able to own and apologize for how I was acting. I shared with Jeff that I realized it would be hard for me to change until we arrived at the gate and knew we would make our flight. I confessed that I wanted to change and that I was working on trusting the Lord in the moment. This admission changed the tension that was happening between us and brought a sense of closeness between Jeff and me.

The other arrow on the Enneagram symbol is pointing to our Growth Path. Again, using myself as an example, Type 9s (Peaceful Mediators) move to the healthy attributes of a Type 3, (Successful Achievers).

I'll share a little "behind the scenes" with you on how growth has led me to access the healthy side of Type 3.

You see, Type 9s normally feel that their presence and voice don't matter to the world, and we struggle to develop ourselves and our self-confidence. When I trust in the Gospel, I realize I do matter to the Lord and can truly bless others if I am willing to assert myself and follow my calling. This kind of growth is not easy, but with the Lord, it is possible. My growth also brings him glory, blesses others, and brings me great joy. Accessing this Type 3 confidence assures me I have something to offer.

So, when I felt the Lord tugging on my heart to share about the Enneagram, which had helped me so much, I decided to go for it and trust him to hold my hand through the parts that were uncomfortable. I stepped out in faith, and he stepped with me!

I remember the first time I had to get in front of a group to talk about the Enneagram. My hands were sweaty, and I felt like I wanted to throw up. (Seriously, that may be oversharing, but it's 100 percent accurate for how I felt!) But Type 3s usually love taking the stage and being in front of people. They can take command of an audience and are usually never more comfortable than when they're sharing what they've learned or entertaining others.

This is how I accessed Type 3 for my own growth. Once I got in front of the group and began to pass on what I had learned, I relaxed and was able to communicate well. I can even say that now I enjoy speaking to groups!

That's why understanding how the Lines and Arrows work is so useful to be able to step back and evaluate what's going on inside us and look at how we are accessing other Types. Looking at our areas of stress and growth helps us to use the Enneagram GPS to know where we're going and to give some checks and balances to our hearts.

To keep this easy to understand, I've chosen to highlight what we are like when we are accessing our Type's Stress Path and Growth Path, but we also access the positive and negatives of both the numbers we are connected to, which I call our Blind Spot Path and Transcending Path. Learning how your Type uses all four paths is vital to deep and transformative growth.

There is so much more to learn about accessing and using elements from the Types we are connected to. You can find out more at **YourEnneagramCoach.com**.

Using Our Understanding of the Enneagram to Grow

When we're using the Enneagram to shine a light on our heart's desires and motivations, how do we know when we are heading in the right direction?

Above all else, we need to pray and ask the Holy Spirit to illuminate our heart (Eph. 1:17–18). Remember, the Bible says our hearts are deceitful, so we truly need the Holy Spirit's guidance. He will reveal to us what we need to see and surrender in the right timing; therefore, we can trust him as we walk this often-rocky internal journey.

It's not always easy for us to become aware of how our heart is doing. It takes a great deal of time and intentional focus. But we can start by first observing our inner world from a *non-judgmental* stance. (I don't know how to emphasize this enough!) We need to remind ourselves of Romans 8:1, which says, "There is therefore now no condemnation for those who are in Christ Jesus." When we're not judging ourselves and resting in the finished work of Christ on our behalf, we're able to see ourselves more clearly. Only then can we learn more about ourselves so we can know when our heart is aligned, misaligned, or out of alignment with the Gospel.

Then we can begin to recognize patterns being awakened by our rumble strips, pause (if only for a nanosecond) while we are in the present circumstance, and ask ourselves good, clarifying questions about *why* we are thinking, feeling, or behaving in particular ways, whether positively or negatively. We can begin to identify those frustrating patterns that we repeat over and over again (the ones we haven't been able to figure out how to stop!) and begin to think about why we keep doing them!

The more we're able to understand the inclinations of our heart, the more we can bring ourselves to God, thank him for delivering us, and ask him to make us more like Christ. "For the grace of God has appeared, bringing salvation for all people, training us to renounce ungodliness and worldly passions, and to live self-controlled, upright, and godly lives in the present age, waiting for our blessed hope, the appearing of the glory of our great God and Savior Jesus Christ, who gave himself for us to redeem us from all lawlessness and to purify for himself a people for his own possession who are zealous for good works" (Titus 2:11–14).

We can also pray specifically for our spouse in their Type and see how we can encourage, support, and even cheer them on when they are growing in likeness in Christ.

If we're willing to take off our lens for just a moment and try to see through their lens, then we will gain a whole new understanding and empathy. Knowing their Type and choosing to look through their lens instead of our own allows us to see them in a way we may have never seen them before.

This one (not simple but incredibly effective) modification in how we relate to one another will completely change the dynamics in our relationships. We're doing more than "walking in their shoes." We're understanding what motivates them and why they're doing what they're doing. And, hopefully, that understanding inclines our heart toward compassion and the desire to extend grace.

And this is the functional definition of grace, for us and for those we love. Grace is the free and unmerited favor of God, and if we can show that same unconditional love to ourselves and our spouse, we can radically change our relationships for the better.

CHAPTER 5:

Childhood Messages

Our Past is Never Really Past

Jeff

Beth and I hadn't been married very long when one day she said to me, "Jeff, I don't know how to be your wife."

If you've been married for any length of time, you're aware that your past shows up at your doorstep when you least expect it. Any thought or event that happens can activate a memory or a sensation in your body.

As we shared earlier, Beth was struggling because she didn't feel her contributions to our marriage and home had any value. I was basically still taking care of myself. I didn't rely on her, or anyone else, only myself. I would clean, cook, wash my laundry, and do whatever else needed to get done around the house. I didn't think twice about it.

All the things I was doing were basically good things. But she felt left out, and rightly so.

I actually couldn't tell her what was going on, because I didn't know. I didn't know why I was shutting her out, but I had a feeling it was tied to my past.

Understanding the present often relies on understanding the past. We can't reinterpret current circumstances if we're unable or unwilling to understand *why* we originally created the first interpretation.

Taking a step back and looking at some of the messages we picked up as children and how our personality interpreted them helped Beth and me better understand why we were responding the way we were in our current predicament as a couple.

In my childhood story, I remember making my first meatloaf for me and my dad when I was in third grade. Because of my mom's illness, she would sometimes need to stay at the hospital several times a year. As I grew older, I was often left alone to take care of myself while my dad worked to support us and visit Mom in the hospital. I needed to grow up fast, take responsibility, and be able to look after myself. I knew how to cook and do my laundry in third grade. I was able to care for myself. I didn't need anyone, nor did I see a reason to rely on anyone else.

When we got married, it didn't even cross my mind to depend on Beth for anything. My Type 6 perspective had always been that I needed to be responsible, dutiful, and hardworking to ensure my security and well-being.

That's why, after a couple years of marriage, Beth began to wonder, "Does Jeff even need me?" This thought translated into her Type 9 heart as a validation that her presence didn't matter. It was hard for her to know how to love me when I had trouble allowing her to show me love.

In Beth's childhood story, her mom was a stay-at-home mom until Beth went to middle school. Her mom faithfully supported the family by driving everyone around, getting the groceries, dry cleaning, doing the laundry, cooking the meals, and keeping the house tidy. Beth's vision of a loving wife was to support and care for her husband… but I didn't need that vision from her. This discrepancy left her feeling inadequate, like she didn't matter, and wondering what her role was as a wife.

Beth and I each interpreted the relational dynamics of our family of origin from the perspective of our Enneagram Types, along with our Childhood Messages.

Our different family dynamics, along with our different personality Type's perspectives, would often create the perfect storm for committing "assumicide." When we didn't understand our childhoods and our Type's perspectives, we allowed our assumptions to run wild, which ultimately caused us to commit "assumicide" time and time again, wreaking havoc in our relationship. We were each separately convinced that our own perspectives on life were accurate and right, and the solution was for the *other* person to change and think like us.

We didn't know there were other ways of interpreting life and circumstances besides our own.

But since that time, I have worked to know my own story and also to know Beth's story. I realized I needed to look at circumstances not just from my viewpoint but also from Beth's. I needed to get to know her and her story on a deeper level in order to know when truth was leading us and when we were both being pulled into lies from our past or misconceptions from our personality's hardwiring.

This revelation started a long and sometimes difficult journey inward, but the rewards were bountiful. I really got to know Beth. I got to know her fears, desires, pains, and longings. I got to understand *why* she reacted in particular ways.

And we came up with some tools to help each other understand what would be helpful and identify what would be harmful when we got stuck. (And we're both happy sharing the housework together now!)

Ignoring our past lets it sneak up on us and wreak all sorts of havoc.

But intentionally looking at our past through the lens of the Enneagram with the guidance of the Gospel makes us aware of the motivations behind what we are doing so we can realize that our past has an impact, wanted or not.

Now a word of warning: This is where moderation comes in. Too much focus on the past can be detrimental. And too little focus on the past can leave us with blinders on.

Dan Allender says it this way, "If you want to create a different future, you must have the courage to look at the past."

Perhaps God intends to prove his faithfulness in our lives by helping us to understand our past better so we can be more fully present in our marriage and set a healthier course together for the future.

Childhood Messages and Core Longings for Each Enneagram Type

Beth

From the moment of our birth, we are constantly listening, learning, and interpreting the world.

Most Enneagram teachers believe we are born our particular Type, and then when we are adults (or in our upper teens) we can discover our Type since we are better able to understand our heart's

Core Motivations. When we determine our Type, it makes all the pieces of the puzzle fit together.

In essence, we are born "hardwired" toward one particular personality Type—our main Type, which holds our Core Motivations (*why* we do what we do). That means that even as small children, we are seeing the world through the lens of our Type even though we didn't know it at the time. To children, our perception of life was reality and accurate. We didn't know there were other ways to see and interpret the same circumstances.

To help understand this concept, let's imagine a family having nine children, each with a different main Enneagram Type. Since they are all from one family, each of them experiences the same circumstances yet each perceives and interprets those same circumstances differently since they each have a different lens or perspective on life. This explains why people are so perplexed when their siblings didn't "experience" the same event in the same way they did. Each person is convinced that they perceived and interpreted the event correctly and everyone else is wrong or downright "crazy."

A dear mentor and friend of ours, Dr. Robert Davis Smart, wisely said, "Children are wonderful observers but often horrible interpreters." This is so true. (Again, we're talking about typical childhood experiences, as opposed to abusive or traumatic ones.) We need to realize that we interpreted our childhood through one particular perspective and that particular interpretation, whether accurate or not, can continue to influence us as adults, especially if left unexamined.

It's important to mention that although we believe, like other Enneagram teachers, that we were all born as our main Type and we're on a journey to discover it, it is *essential* that parents and adults not "Type" children since children are still in the process of figuring out their world and mirroring their parents and other authority figures.

This mirroring makes it challenging to know what a child's Type is even if their habits and mannerisms may look suspiciously like a particular Type. Actually, we can't "Type" them (or anyone else) since it is impossible for us to know their inner world and Core Motivations. Only they can reveal this when they are older since it takes time for any person to be able to understand their heart well enough to know which Type reflects their Core Fear, Desire, and Longing.

Be curious, but never tell someone their Type. Let them discover it for themselves.

As adults, we can find it enormously helpful to look back on our childhood, (particularly when we know our Enneagram Type) to help us further understand why we interpreted events in a particular way. It is also beneficial to see if we interpreted events correctly or misinterpreted them based on our understanding of our Type's perspective and interpretations. This new awareness will also enable us to see how our Type's perspective is still impacting us as adults and the stories we tell ourselves.

What Is the Childhood Message?

Our "Childhood Message" is the message we were either told directly or we sensed and interpreted from life circumstances through the lens of our personality Type. This message was (and still is) painful to us. It greatly impacted us as children and still does to this day as adults. It is important for us to know what this message is and how it is hardwired into our thinking so we can bring the healing truth of the Gospel to our hearts and live more freely in Christ's messages for us.

There's not always a direct correlation to a particular event that happened in our childhood; sometimes, but not always. Yet, somewhere, somehow, we picked up a message that internally rang true for us (accurate or not) due to our Type. We can see how each

Enneagram Type has a perspective through which we saw life as children. Gaining insight into how your personality Type interpreted events and relationships in childhood will help you to identify how that interpretation is impacting you today. What's more, when you know the Childhood Message of your Type and you know your spouse's Type, you can then begin to gain some insights into why they do what they do and how you can understand and communicate with them more effectively.

As we said, the Childhood Message is a message that is already hardwired in our personality from birth, and we interpret circumstances based off this message. Our parents, teachers, and authority figures may have directly communicated this message to us, but most of the time, we interpreted what they said or did to fit this hardwiring belief. Believing this false interpretation or message only constrains us and causes our personality to reinforce its strategies to protect us from our Core Fear.

There are three kinds of childhood messages.

1. **Wounding Messages** arrive with an intent to harm (or perceived harm).
2. **Injuring Messages** result from something harmful that happens with no ill intent.
3. **Influencing Messages** arrive with the intent to shape or guide.

Let's take a simple illustration of a child who has done something wrong and is being sent to "time-out" and look at various responses to that situation. For now, please don't overthink this illustration since we are not trying to focus on the pros and cons of disciplining children but instead how each Type could experience or interpret a "time-out" differently.

Remember, our purpose here is to focus specifically on marriage even though we are talking about children and childhood memories;

we will *not* be addressing parenting issues here. We'll save that for another time.

In this "time-out" illustration:

- A **wounding message** would come when a child is being intentionally left alone with no intent to go back and check on them. If you know the Harry Potter series, think of Harry's uncle Vernon Dursley, who locked Harry in a closet! The uncle's intent was not to correct and care for Harry but to be mean and punish.
- An **injuring message** might be a child being sent to their room for time-out and "think about what they had done" and accidentally getting forgotten (yes, it happens to the best of us!). Though the intent wasn't to forget them, it just happened, and the child felt injured because of it.
- An **influencing message** might be a child being sent to a "quiet" place to help them stop what they were doing that was inappropriate. They may feel alone at the time, but when they reconnect, they are reassured that their time-out was for a purpose and they are loved and cherished.

We'll get back to this illustration in a bit.

First, let's address the childhood wounds. If you have childhood wounds (things that happened intentionally to harm you) and you need to process that trauma, we strongly recommend that you find a professional to walk you through what happened.

And a child could have perceived harm and been wounded or injured, even if no overt harm was inflicted. Again, if something causes you great pain and impacts your relationships, we strongly encourage you to get professional help.

But our focus here is to look at ways we interpret more general events that happened to us as children and to see how we interpreted these events through our Type's hardwiring or "Childhood Message." We also want to see how this message still impacts us today.

Here are the Childhood Messages that are hardwired into each Type. We were either directly told, or thought were being told to us, through our Type's interpretation of events:

- **1's:** "It's not okay to be wrong or make mistakes."
- **2's:** "It's not okay to have needs of your own."
- **3's:** "It's not okay for you to have your own feelings and identity."
- **4's:** "It's not okay to be too much and not enough."
- **5's:** "It's not okay to be comfortable in the world."
- **6's:** "It's not okay to trust or depend on yourself."
- **7's:** "It's not okay to depend on others for anything."
- **8's:** "It's not okay to trust or be vulnerable with anyone."
- **9's:** "It's not okay to assert yourself or think much of yourself."

Do you see the power and harm these beliefs hold? How did your Type's Childhood Message impact you and how is it still impacting your life? How did your spouse's Type's Childhood Message impact them and how is it still impacting their life?

Core Longing (Message Your Heart Longed to Hear)

In many ways, your Core Longing (the message your heart longs to hear) is what you yearned to hear while you were young. As a child, you craved and thirsted to hear this message, yet no matter how much you tried to get others to communicate it to you, you never felt it was communicated *to the degree* your heart needed it.

The reason you never felt deeply satisfied when others tried to communicate this Core Longing to you is that people cannot adequately give you all that you need. Only God can and he completely communicates this message to your heart through the finished work of Christ.

The problem is that we want it in some tangible form. We wanted our parents to fully communicate this to us so it would feel real and true. Since no parent is perfect, and they couldn't give it to us in the deep and substantial way we craved, we believed it wasn't true and left us seeking and craving it throughout all our life. We brought this Core Longing into our marriage and family, which has greatly impacted how we relate and sense the other person's love.

We don't believe our spouse loves us to the degree we need since they have not completely communicated or satisfied this Core Longing within us to the degree that we crave. Therefore, we continue to search for it and try to earn it but are always left unsatisfied.

This is why we must turn back to the Spring of Living Water (Jer. 2:13) who replenishes and satisfies our Core Longing. He provides all we need so that when others try to offer it to us, we can feel it since we are already filled up and satisfied by Christ filling us up. We are no longer desperate and demanding others come through for us in ways they cannot. We can receive and believe others the more we receive and believe our Core Longing has been fulfilled by Christ.

The **Core Longing** (message a child's heart longs to hear) for each Type is:

- **1's:** "You are good."
- **2's:** "You are wanted and loved."
- **3's:** "You are loved and valued for simply being you."
- **4's:** "You are seen and loved for exactly who you are."
- **5's:** "Your needs are not a problem."
- **6's:** "You are safe and secure."
- **7's:** "You will be taken care of."
- **8's:** "You will not be betrayed."
- **9's:** "Your presence matters."

Do you recognize the message your heart longed to hear as a child? Do you see how you still long for it to be communicated to you? How does this impact your life now? Do you find yourself trying to earn it or hear it from your spouse and others? How would your heart be freed if this was communicated to you in such a deep way that it truly impacted your heart?

Now put your spouse's lens on and recognize the message their heart longed to hear as a child. Do you see how they still long for it to be communicated to them today? How does this impact their life now? Do they still try to earn it or hear it from you and others? How would their heart be freed if this were communicated to them in such a deep way their heart could hear and receive it?

Back to our "time-out" illustration…

Let's see how the Childhood Message and Core Longing might have impacted each child differently by looking again at our "time-out" situation. And let's assume there was no ill intent (or wounding message) and the child was mistakenly forgotten.

- A **Type 1** child might surmise they were "bad" and that's why they were forgotten.
- A **Type 2** child might feel unloved and unwanted.
- A **Type 3** child might feel someone else was worthier than them of attention.
- A **Type 4** child might not feel like they were special enough to deserve attention.
- A **Type 5** child might think their needs were a problem to be forgotten about.
- A **Type 6** child might think no one was going to come and rescue them, leaving them abandoned.
- A **Type 7** child might think they can't depend on anyone.
- A **Type 8** child might surmise it's not okay to trust anyone since they were forgotten (harmed or betrayed).

- A **Type 9** child might believe they just didn't matter since they were overlooked and forgotten.

The Enneagram can shed light on why we saw our upbringing from a particular perspective. Each Type will react to the same circumstances in different ways. Just like we said earlier, if a family had nine children and each child had a different personality Type, then they would all perceive and interpret the same circumstances differently, because they see life through different colored lenses. Each child will be activated due to their Core Motivation and will therefore react in ways that align to their personality's defense strategies. Some will withdraw. Some will fight. Some will comply.

Knowing your personality Type and studying your childhood patterns will greatly help you to see through a new lens so you can begin to break free from patterns that have kept you stuck personally and in your marriage.

As you learn more about your personality Type and learn more about your spouse's personality Type, you can begin to see how each impacted childhood perceptions, perceptions you may still carry today. It will allow you to reinterpret, and even rewrite, pieces of your story now that you have a better perspective and vantage point. Because when you were a young child, you were just trying to make sense of life and what you were observing.

When looking back, please be gracious to yourself, your spouse, and your past. Be understanding, sensitive, nonjudgmental, caring, and supportive. And remember, there's only one person who can fully redeem our past—Jesus. He can free you from the chains that bind, restoring you to a new freedom found only in him.

How to Learn from the Past

The term "family of origin" refers to the family that raised you—your parents and siblings. It may also include a grandparent, other relatives, or stepparents if your parents were divorced and you lived with them during part of your childhood.

As we look back at our childhoods and begin to understand its impact on us through the Enneagram, we find another opportunity to be an "observer."

We know that not everyone has a "perfect family" story. We are deeply saddened that there are many horrific childhood stories that remind us of how fallen our world is and how much harm can happen to children.

But remember, for our purposes here, we are not going to focus on childhood trauma per se; we're just going to explore how we *perceived* our childhoods.

What does it look like to address our own story safely with honesty and compassion?

As we remember and reflect on our childhood, here are some guidelines:

- Be sure to share your story with "safe" people. Safe people are curious, kind, and gentle. If you cannot safely share your story with anyone around you, seek a professional counselor, therapist, or pastor.
- Be careful of *how* you talk to yourself. Reflection is not a time for "should" or "ought." We may *wish* for a different story, but we can't change the past. We can only reflect in the present to become who we were meant to be in the future.
- The intent of visiting our past is to focus on how we interpreted events. The goal is not to address the situations with our family members. Don't be quick to confront people (especially parents or siblings) about your story. They may have had a different experience, or you may raise issues they're not ready to confront. Again, if past issues

need resolution, it may be time to seek professional help for guidance.

Often, we choose interpretations of our past that justify our current way of relating. We want to be curious enough about how we see our world so as to differentiate between helpful and harmful ways of relating that originated in our family of origin but may be negatively impacting our present relationships.

So, what does this thinking about your Childhood Message look like?

- **Be honest about the past.** Many families do try to reinterpret past events in a positive light, perhaps even from the perspective of their Types, but your perceptions of what happened and how you viewed life through the lens of your Type and your experience are important.
- **Be honest about the effects of the past.** It mattered. Some real pain and betrayal may have impacted how you view the world. All families have complexity in their interactions and family dynamics.
- **Be honest about your interpretation of past events.**

When we become adults, we often are not aware of how our Childhood Message influenced us. When we get into a marital relationship, we usually bring those same interpretations into our marriages, and so we need to ask ourselves clarifying questions to find out:

- How did I see it? And was what I perceived as reality actually what happened?
- How can I gain clarity and understanding now as an adult?
- How can I understand how circumstances impacted me?
- How do similar circumstances still impact me today since my Childhood Message has felt accurate all these years?

- How can I bring the truth of the Gospel into my life and free me from a wrong interpretation of events?

Take some time to process how you saw circumstances. Be gentle with yourself and allow God's unending love to wash over you and free you.

The Impact of Childhood Messages

Jeff

I didn't fully understand the impact of our Childhood Messages and how differently Beth and I approached life until we were in the middle of a fight about ten years into our marriage. Beth, from her Type 9 perspective, thought we were "fighting," and I assumed what we were doing was "arguing." (Fighting being destructive and arguing being an expression of opposing ideas and feelings.)

Regardless of what we each thought was happening, Beth and I were in our typically unhelpful "dance." We were at it *again*. It didn't even matter what we were fighting about, because the dance itself was the same no matter what the problem was.

I was actually following her around the house talking "at" her. (If I couldn't connect, I would rather argue than have silence since Type 6s fear being abandoned and alone. I desperately felt the need for her to engage with me.) This particular fight started in the kitchen, and then Beth, in her frustration, went into our bedroom.

Wanting to resolve the disagreement, I followed her to the bedroom. I'm a fairly passionate person under the best of circumstances, and in times of stress, I can get super intense. Beth, feeling like things were going nowhere, just wanted to retreat and deal with things "later" (a typical Type 9 pattern of avoiding conflict and tension is to withdraw or avoid). We were not getting anywhere. We just continued to trip over each other and painfully step on each other's toes.

When Beth closed the door to our bedroom, a very familiar, deep fear was building in my heart. I wondered (as I often did when there was conflict between us), "Is this the beginning of the end? Is Beth going to leave me?"

But this is where the Enneagram is incredibly helpful for understanding context.

The roots of my fear come from my Type 6, the Loyal Guardian's perspective of life. My Core Fear has to do with abandonment, insecurity, and being alone. Abandonment is a fear I have carried with me for a very long time. I always knew I was adopted, and my parents were very open about adopting me. But at times I felt a lack of discipline and engagement. It wasn't their fault; much was due to my mother's chronic illness.

Although I always knew my adoptive parents loved me, their disengagement at times felt to me like abandonment. I probably wouldn't have named it as abandonment growing up or in my young adulthood. But it was through Beth's study of the Enneagram that I started to understand and recognize that my fear of abandonment had always been a part of my life's perspective—an awareness that, for me, was heightened by my Type 6 perspective rather than my adoption since other adoptees of different Types would view their adoption differently.

Since my parents were overwhelmed with life and my mom's chronic illness, I began thinking my needs were too much, I was too much, and my problems were way too big.

(From the perspective of the Enneagram, you can see that other Types would have responded differently under the same circumstances. For example, a Type 1 may have thought their parents didn't have strong enough rules. A Type 3 may have assumed their parents and others only wanted them for their accomplishments, not their true selves. A Type 7 may have assumed no one would fully be able to care for their never-ending needs and desires.)

Because of the way I was "hardwired" as a Type 6 and having my mom not always available due to being sick (which caused my dad to often need to be focused more on her), I have felt "on my own" my entire life. Don't get me wrong. My parents were present and involved with me, but from my Type 6's perspective, I truly felt like I was responsible for myself from the time I was about five years old.

As I grew up, I brought into all my relationships the Type 6's Core Fear that I don't want to be abandoned. Deep down, fear nagged at me that the other person in my relationships would leave and I would, once again, be alone and left to fend for myself.

So, when Beth and I were in the midst of this awful fight (yet again), that deep-rooted, gnawing Core Fear raised its ugly head.

In that moment, when she retreated to our bedroom, my heart dropped, and I felt my insecurity rising.

I went into the bedroom and Beth was on the bed crying and not saying anything (her typical pattern as a Type 9 who fears conflict). I started yelling again as I somehow thought that the louder I got, the more likely it was that she would come back, connect, "return fire," or engage with me in some way because that's what I would have done in a similar situation.

Getting no response from her, I was about to storm out of the room and slam the door when I felt a "rumble strip" in my heart that made me aware of a habitual pattern. I knew Type 6's at their core were often scared of being left, and the Holy Spirit gave me pause.

I actually walked out of the room and then came back in. Realizing I couldn't get through to her by yelling, and we were at an impasse, I took a deep breath, and with my heart in my throat, I simply and quietly asked a very vulnerable (clarifying) question, "Are you going to leave me?"

She looked at me in disbelief at first, and then with an understanding look and puffy eyes, she said, "Seriously??? No, stupid! I won't *ever* leave you. I am all in. I love you and I'm fully committed to you. *That's who I am.*"

Her raw and authentic words penetrated my heart. I got it.

I held her for what felt like hours and through tears, we connected. In that moment, I realized I bring a fear that is *not real* into all my relationships. My Type 6, with my childhood messages, led me to a place where I was committing "assumicide" and it was actually destroying my relationship with Beth. When I paused and assessed what was going on through my Type 6 lens, I realized I could make a choice not to react in a "knee-jerk" kind of way, and I could stop and ask a question to clarify what was really happening.

Looking back, two major shifts happened in me during that awful fight with Beth in our bedroom.

First, I now know that if my heart is at rest with the promise that Jesus will never "leave me nor forsake me," I can survive whatever is thrown at me—I will never be abandoned by him. And fortunately, in Beth's love for me, my fear of her leaving me was ungrounded.

But second, by being aware of what was going on inside me, I could make some different (and better) choices to become more aligned with myself and the Gospel. I could ask the deeply vulnerable questions that my heart was wrestling with and know that, no matter what the answers were, I would be okay.

In that moment, I also understood for the first time that I was truly seeing and relating to the world in a completely different way than Beth. *That's not who she is.*

Right there in the doorway of our bedroom, with the help of the Enneagram, I grew closer to Jesus and my wife. The realization of my fear of abandonment did not heap shame on me. Instead, it invited me to trust God and to experience a connection with my wife in a new (and more secure) way.

CHAPTER **6:**

Communication

—

Beth

Our friends Ken (Type 7, the Entertaining Optimist) and Jeanette (Type 6, the Loyal Guardian) have a healthy marriage, but it isn't without communication mishaps. Ken's an exuberant Type 7 who's fun, loving, and spontaneous. He loves parties and celebrations, and when he's having a difficult day at work, he can occasionally be found walking aimlessly through a local department store looking for something to purchase as "retail therapy"—shopping being the source of all things new and exciting.

Jeanette, on the other hand, is a 6 who loves to be practical and responsible. She prides herself on being frugal. She could be a poster child for Dave Ramsey's *EveryDollar* budget tool!

Christmas was fast approaching, and Ken and Jeanette scheduled a date night to shop for family and friends. The chill in the air made it feel all the more like Christmas. The downtown shopping area, decorated with wreaths, holly, and mistletoe, looked like it could be the set of a Hallmark movie… but it became a beautiful backdrop for a marital fight instead.

As they began to shop, Ken excitedly began the search to find the most fascinating and interesting gifts for the people on their list. Jeanette pulled out her (printed) shopping list and said they should focus *only* on "The List" and *only* on what a person wanted or needed.

Ken didn't understand why she was so focused on "practical" when the *true* heart of Christmas was about celebration, given the "reason for the season." He refused to buy anything other than something the person didn't know they needed or the latest, greatest, or most interesting gift. Christmas was all about the surprise and the unexpected. Jeanette doggedly refused to get something "extravagant" and ridiculous.

They were stopped in the middle of the sidewalk at an impasse. Neither one of them wanted to back off. They decided to continue shopping, but there was a palpable tension between them. They decided to split up, and he left to buy a few "off the list" gifts, while she hunted for "socks and underwear" types of gifts. They ended up going home in silence, feeling frustrated and put out with each other. The evening didn't turn out to be the fun holiday date night they had planned.

When they got home, they were both still a little annoyed, but they decided to try to talk about what happened before they went to bed.

They sat in the kitchen and when their hearts were both prepared to talk (not reactive or defensive), Ken began by asking a clarifying question. He said to Jeanette, "I stopped to think about it, and I'd actually really like to understand what was going on. Can you explain to me what you think happened? What was going on in your heart so I can better understand you?"

Jeanette thought about it and then calmly explained how, when she was growing up, her dad struggled with employment, and their funds were super tight. "Wish lists" weren't a reality. So she always wanted to get *exactly* what people wanted on their lists, even if it was practical… actually, especially if it was practical. Jeanette had never shared that particular piece of information with Ken before (she actually hadn't really thought of it before they started talking), and he was surprised by it.

Ken said, "Really? I didn't realize that. That makes sense."

Jeanette asked him, "So what was going on with you? It felt unreasonable to me, but I think there was more to it."

Ken then explained that nothing brought him more happiness than to do something "out of the box" and exciting for those he loved. He said that for him, because his mother had a disability, when he did something unexpected and fun for her, she would laugh and be happy. It made *him* happy to bring her joy, particularly when she struggled with pain so much. He loved doing that same kind of thing for others so they could feel joy, too. "Socks and underwear" just didn't have the same effect.

Jeanette said she hadn't thought of it that way… but maybe they could figure something out that would work for both of them.

At the beginning of the New Year, they were working on the family budget (thank you, Dave Ramsey), and they came up with a workable compromise. They planned two budgets for Christmas… a "practical" budget for her and a "Type 7 fun" budget for him.

Because Ken and Jeanette asked each other clarifying questions and were open to hearing what was going on with each other at a heart level, they were better able to understand the "why" behind their conflict. That "why" helped them create a solution that made sense for them, while still respecting each other and their personality Types.

Our hearts can get activated (or triggered) in situations when we least expect it. And when as a couple we are both activated, well, it doubles the potential for misunderstandings!

It's often hard to remember the truth of *who* we are and *Whose* we are, because the false messages from the less-than-healthy parts of our personalities are so intense and can arise instantly. If we react immediately, we can get upset, irritable, accusatory, sad, withdrawn, passive, or aggressive. We're usually flooded with thoughts and feelings, and we usually don't stop to ask questions. We just react.

But, gratefully, we have ways to break the cycle! The best way to break the cycle is to ask clarifying questions. But before we can ask those questions, we need to do one thing first…

And that is to pause, for a moment, and listen to the Holy Spirit and our "rumble strip" warnings inside us.

We start by remembering *who we are and Whose we are.* Christ loves us fully, and he is there to guide, love, and provide for us even if others do not give us what our heart desires. He fulfills us completely, even when others deplete us. He protects us even when others don't understand us.

In the moment we take to pause, with the help of the Holy Spirit, we can allow him to give us new ways of communicating that alter our communication dynamics in a way that honors and glorifies him. The Spirit enables me to ask clarifying questions like, "Here's what I think is going on… but before I make an assumption about it, I want to ask you first. Can you explain to me what was going on and why you did what you did so I can better understand your perspective?"

When I ask from a genuine heart, I can handle the conversation and outcome with more love and ease. By going about the conversation this way, I make sure I understand more of what's going on.

The majority of the time, I have found that if my husband knows that I *truly* want to know him, hear him, and understand him, he's willing to extend the same grace to me. But when I am reactive and committing assumicide, then all that grace flies out the window, and fights and arguments begin.

I have to do my own internal work. I first have to come back to the truth of the Gospel and who I am in Christ before anything else happens. After I am grounded there, I often have to share with my husband the messages that are constantly floating inside me. (For some reason, he still hasn't learned to read my mind!) My sharing helps him to know how to love me better and to understand how I can so quickly get activated by misinterpreting circumstances that deliver powerful yet false messages.

It's not Jeff's job to fix me or rescue me. Only Christ can do that. But my husband can come alongside me and communicate in ways that help my heart to remain on the right path. I can also do the same for him when I understand what activates his heart to believe his false messages. We can be there for each other.

So, as we wrestle with the core lies that entangle our hearts, let us love one another, serve one another, and lift one another up to bring the truth of the Gospel back into our hearts. Let us spur one another on in all our communication for his ultimate glory and our joy.

Our Words and Our Hearts

Jeff

When we think about "communication," we often think just about the words that we speak. But our words come from our hearts.

"For out of the abundance of the heart, the mouth speaks" (Matt. 12:34). Our heart's intent is more important than just our words. Christ warns specifically about focusing on outward behaviors and instructs them to clean their internal world first so the outside may also stay clean. "Woe to you, teachers of the law and Pharisees, you hypocrites! You clean the outside of the cup and dish, but inside they are full of greed and self-indulgence" (Matt. 23:25–26).

We may try to change our vocabulary. We may even try to refrain from speaking. But unless our hearts are transformed, our efforts are futile.

When it comes to communicating with our spouse, we may be tempted to think, "If I could just understand what he is talking about…" or "If only she understood what I meant…" then we would have a great marriage." But as most of us know, words alone don't always lead to understanding when we're determined to be the correct one.

Each of the Enneagram Types has their own communication style. Each Type communicates in a style that reflects their Core Motivations. So, when a Type perceives any of their Core Motivations are true (or might come true), they internally become activated (positively or negatively) and their particular communication style will follow accordingly.

When we perceive that our Core Fear is coming true, we'll communicate in a way that reflects our heart to protect ourselves. The problem is that our assumptions and perceptions may be skewed or inaccurate, which means we can react in ways that are not always warranted and can even be harmful.

When we commit "assumicide" and do not ask good clarifying questions, we react in ways that can be confusing and hurtful to our spouse. These hurtful situations can escalate very quickly into a major conflict or fight that is not helpful or productive.

If we are not self-aware or even situationally aware (meaning that you can tell by your spouse's body language or non-verbal cues that something is wrong), we can find ourselves reacting in unhelpful ways.

When communication slides off the rails, we tend to find our hearts veering off course where we end up in the same pitfall time after time.

Ken Sande, who wrote *The Peacemaker: A Biblical Guide to Resolving Personal Conflict,* shows us this dangerous path that is also the progression of an idol in our heart. (An idol is anything we put our trust in, give ourselves to, or put our hope in to give us life. An idol impacts our communication when we are seeking to satisfy our heart's core motives at the expense of our spouse.)

- **We desire.** God gives us longings and desires that can be good when communicated well and align with his truth. But when these are not met by our spouse or others, we can find ourselves slipping into the next three pitfalls which reveals the idols in our hearts.
- **We demand.** We attach an expectation to a desire. *"You must do this…"*
- **We judge or criticize.** We go after the person, not the issue. *"If you would only…"*
- **We punish.** We withdraw or attack. (Silence can be as loud as yelling.)

Bids

Let's take this a step further.

John Gottman, PhD, a marriage researcher, has observed something profound about how we act on our desires in his book *The Relationship Cure.* He uses the word "bids" to describe ***any attempt for connection***. Bids can show up both positively and negatively. In order to love our spouse well, we will need to have the tools necessary to understand that behind a negative bid may be a positive *desire*.

Dr. Gottman says that bids can come into your life in an infinite number of ways, some of which are "easy to see and interpret, others that are nearly indecipherable." Bids may be thoughts, feelings, observations, opinions, or invitations. Whether they are verbal or nonverbal, physical, sexual, intellectual, humorous, serious, or in the form of a question, statement, or comment, they qualify as a "bid" for connection.

Here's an example of the same bid in two different ways.

A negative bid: "I guess I will have to take out the trash, again."

A positive bid: "Can you please take out the trash?"

Both are bids for connection. They just come across very differently!

It is crucial for us to know what our heart's desires are and first rely on God being the real source of our fulfillment, but then also learning how to communicate our desires to our spouse in a way that is positive without demands, judgments, or punishments. How we communicate with our words, actions, and body language are crucial to the overall health of our relationship to our spouse.

Thriving spouses turn toward their spouses' bid for connection whether the bid is negative or positive—the point is, there is connection.

Equally so, as a spouse reaches for us, understanding how their communication style has been impacted by their Enneagram Type, and how we as our Type react, provides an opportunity to serve one another with every conversation.

But again, we'll be at risk of committing "assumicide" if we don't know what our spouse actually is saying, not just what we believe they are saying.

Clarifying Questions are simply questions to help establish more fact than just assumptions. They clarify the dilemma and provide confirmation so you can make sure you understand what was intended by the other person. Clarifying Questions are an excellent way to help you avoid committing "assumicide."

Here are some examples of **Clarifying Questions**.

Start with: Can you clarify for me what you meant so I don't assume incorrectly?

- Is this what you said…? (Repeat back what you heard)
- Did I hear you say…? (Repeat back to them)
- Are you saying…? (Repeat back what you heard)
- Did I understand you correctly when you said…? (Repeat, confirm)
- Did I understand you to say…? (Repeat, confirm)
- Could you say it again in another way? (Confirm)
- When I repeated what I said back to you, was it correct? (Confirm)

Here are some questions that are intended to help you get more information. They are open-ended questions avoiding a "yes or no" answer and are typically questions of when, why, and how.

- Could you tell me more about what your fear and/or desire was…?
- What led you to think/believe…?
- What did you mean when you said…?
- What do you think/believe would happen if…?
- How did you decide/determine…?
- What made you think that…?

- How did you come to that conclusion...?
- Why do you think...?
- Tell me more...

Remember, when we don't know something or are not sure of something, we often unintentionally "make it up" in our heads. Clarifying questions can help us determine if what we think we know is actually true... and decrease the chance for misunderstanding.

Change Can Happen

Jeff

As Beth was reading and learning about the Enneagram, I have to admit, I was a little slower to embrace it!

I had always tried to encourage her and support her, but it never seemed like what I was doing was right. The thing was, I didn't really know what was right. I used a lot of "mental analysis" and "trial and error" to make her happy and help her feel secure. I did all the things for her that helped *me, as a Type 6,* to feel happy and secure, but somehow, I always seemed to miss the mark (since what she needed wasn't what a Type 6 needed).

After Beth started learning about the Enneagram, I began to notice that she seemed a little less "desperate." She seemed more content in herself, and she didn't always respond in the ways that she used to (and ways that never seemed particularly helpful). But I was still not convinced of the reason why.

Part of my reluctance to embrace the Enneagram came from my own process of discovery. Initially, when reading about the Enneagram, I thought I was a Type 8 (even though Beth always suspected I was a Type 6). It seemed right. I'd be proud to be known as a Type 8.

Finding my Type felt like trying on a new pair of shoes that can take a while to "break in." But sometimes, those new shoes are actually the wrong fit. I actually wore my wrong Enneagram Type "shoes" for a couple years, and they kept rubbing me the wrong way.

It makes sense that I was hesitant to embrace the whole structure because it didn't quite fit me (and this can happen to a lot of people).

As Beth started learning more and we began seeing a counselor familiar with the Enneagram, that counselor (with lots of grace) led me toward looking at the Type 6, the Loyal Guardian. Quite frankly, that Type made me a little uncomfortable, which I now realize can be indicative of a "good fit"!

Once I landed there, the pieces all seemed to fall into place. Some of my issues around being adopted factored in, and some of the dynamics around my mother's health issues also came into play. And becoming "self-aware" was a process for me, not a one-shot "aha" experience.

But once I was aware of my Type, the process of becoming self-aware started to make a positive impact on my life, both spiritually and relationally.

When Beth and I had a conflict, I was able to pause and think through the lens of the Enneagram about why I was reacting the way I was. And that ability to pause and reflect had tremendous power and benefit. Instead of just reacting to her instinctively, I could make a choice to react differently—more thoughtfully and considerately.

The inverse was also true for how I responded to Beth. When she responded to me in a negative way, I could pause and wonder what was going on with her, instead of just getting defensive and angry. (This change was a huge deal, by the way!)

I, like Beth, assumed I knew where she was coming from and what was motivating her. But after I began to see through the lens of the Enneagram, I actually learned the "secret sauce" for better communication: I learned not to *assume* but to pause, say a quick prayer, and ask her clarifying questions to understand what was going on with her!

And when I listened, I was listening with a different mindset, one that listened for what was going on with *her*, not just what she activated in me.

By listening with intention, I realized it was possible to change for the better and for our relationship to improve in ways I never thought possible before.

Experience Is a Great Teacher

Beth

Learning to communicate better doesn't happen overnight. But with practice, your communication can get better.

Just like learning a new dance, when we first started learning about the Enneagram, we were "stepping on each other's toes" more often than not. But as time went on, Jeff and I began to realize that even though we weren't communicating perfectly, we could find opportunities to apply what we were learning. (Be careful what you wish for!)

As we have shared, Jeff has always been a pastor and that has often meant our budget has usually been extremely limited. Still, I loved decorating our home no matter where we lived to make it feel like a real home. I always wanted to make him happy (one of my Type 9 motivations).

One evening, after a long day at work, my mom came over to help me with a project. I had scrimped and saved, and I bought some fun fabric to make a set of curtains to brighten up our living space.

My mom and I got them made and hung up. They turned out great and were so cute! I waited excitedly to see what Jeff would say about them when he got home from a meeting at church that night.

Jeff got home… and he didn't even notice them! All my hard work to please him was for nothing. My heart sank. I decided to point them out to him and asked, "What do you think?"

He looked up and said, "Umm… nice." and he walked over to check the mail.

My face fell; disappointment was written all over it. Jeff noticed and was confused.

Knowing that I operate differently from him, Jeff paused, thought about me, and wondered what was going on. Then turned to me and with sincerity said, "What are you really asking?"

His genuine concern made me stop and think about my motives. I answered truthfully, "I just want to know if I'm being a good wife!"

He came over and hugged me and said, "You're a great wife. I was distracted and I'm sorry. I really appreciate you and all you do." He smiled and said, "And, actually, the curtains make a big difference… now that I've noticed them!"

Because Jeff had learned to pause and ask clarifying questions and I had learned to examine my internal hidden desires, the two of us could avoid what could have been a bitter fight. We also grew in understanding and love for one another. Because of the Enneagram and its lessons, a misunderstanding that could have spiraled into tension between us instead became one of our favorite memories of a communication breakthrough.

When we first met, all we noticed was how much we had in common; we felt like we were so much alike. And early on in our marriage, all we could see were our differences—and we didn't view those differences positively. We thought those differences were making us miserable, when it was actually how we *viewed* our differences that was making us so unhappy.

That's why it's essential for each of us to recognize, learn, and accept that other people do not see the world the same way we do. As you begin to understand the Enneagram, you can begin to see and understand this truth. When each of us truly begins to comprehend that others see the world from a completely different perspective than ours, we can ask good, clarifying questions that will help us understand more clearly where each person is coming from. Then we will be less likely to make wrong assumptions and damage the relationship by committing "assumicide."

But (and here's where it can get a little dicey) learning the Enneagram isn't primarily about understanding others; it's really about understanding ourselves first—and understanding ourselves at a core level.

We need to understand why we think, feel, and behave the way we do so we can steer our hearts back to Christ. In order to do so, we must ask good, clarifying questions of our own hearts first.

Again, the Lord tells us in Jeremiah 17:9 that the heart is "deceitful above all things, and desperately sick; who can understand it?" Even Paul shares his own internal struggles in Romans 7:15 when he says we do the things we don't want to do and don't do the things we want to do in following the Lord.

We may think we understand ourselves well (some Enneagram Types actually enjoy going deep internally to find out more about themselves), but in my experience as an Enneagram coach, I see that most people struggle to know or understand why they do what they do.

That's why the Enneagram has been so profound for Jeff and me and impacted us so deeply. The Enneagram, in helping us understand our internal world, has brought us clarity so that the Gospel can take root at a deeper level. Through the working of the Holy Spirit, our understanding brings new and rich transformation within us, enabling us to have longer lasting and more beautiful relationships with others, God, and ourselves.

And that's our hope for you as well. Jeff and I are here to be honest, vulnerable, and transparent with you, sharing our story from our darkest days to our most glorious heights so that our story, in God's sovereign plan, provision, love, mercy, and grace, can encourage you in yours.

CHAPTER 7:

Conflict and Hope

Jeff

Dave, a friend of ours, is a pastor of a growing church and longs to have people, especially visitors, experience the beauty and depth of God's love and presence all throughout the worship service. He uses his gifts of intuition, inspiration, and authentic expression to create a unique experience for each person who walks into the church. His hope is that others' emotions will be stirred and elevated in such a way that moves them closer to God and that they will experience genuine hospitality and community while they are there.

His wife, Kelsie, is a high school teacher who does an excellent job "running a tight ship" and developing procedures in her classroom that help her students learn at their best since they always know what is expected of them and how to get their work done correctly. There is no question about what the right way of doing things is in her class. She is very clear and precise.

Dave and Kelsie have been married for ten years and some of the things that attracted them to each other initially seemed now to be creating a wedge between them.

During a season of creative thinking and inspiration, Dave came up with some new and innovative ways to foster a sense of welcome for guests at their church. But when he approached the church leadership, he got way more pushback than he anticipated. He felt frustrated and misunderstood since the church leadership didn't look like they were going to adopt his concepts. They questioned both his vision and his implementation process… which fostered deep-rooted feelings of shame in Dave. The feeling that he was somehow defective and tragically flawed swept over him like a tsunami—bringing feelings that were powerful, overwhelming, and immobilizing.

One night after dinner, Dave told Kelsie what was going on at the church and shared with her some of his feelings of frustration, inadequacy, and shame.

She loved him and wanted to see his vision thrive so she pointed out to him what he would need to do to develop structure, procedures, and a defined method of implementation so the leadership would support him. She laid it all out in a very systematic and detailed way. She was excited to help him and hoped her suggestions would get him out of his funk.

Unfortunately, Dave felt criticized and judged by Kelsie's "helpfulness," deepening his sense of inadequacy. Even after being married for ten years, he felt that she still didn't really understand him.

He felt lonely and unloved and, to protect himself from further emotional distress, he did what came naturally and withdrew into his world of emotions.

Kelsie sensed him retreating into his inner world of emotions. She was getting frustrated that he wouldn't do what she suggested since she knew without a doubt it would be the most effective way for the church leadership to get on board. She didn't understand why he always had to take things so personally when there was a right way of doing everything, and she had clearly laid it out for him.

Finally, she was at the end of her rope.

"Dave, why are you avoiding me?

Reluctantly he said, "When you keep trying to fix the situation, it confirms to me yet again that I'm just not good enough, and it leads me to feel like there's no way you could really love me if I'm that defective and flawed."

"How can you say that? I was simply giving you ways to implement your vision so you wouldn't feel so stuck. But when I try to help you, you pull away and withdraw inwardly as if I were trying to hurt you on purpose. I was *only* trying to help."

Kelsie's frustration and resentment spilled out in her tears and her tone was curt. Dave couldn't see past his emotions and he responded, as was his habit, with silence.

At an impasse, Kelsie went back to working on her lesson plans. And Dave, not knowing what to do, went back to reading his book.

They were, once again, stuck.

It may not be surprising that Dave is a Type 4 and Kelsie is a Type 1.

It's also not surprising that when it comes to conflict and miscommunication, for many couples it sometimes feels like the old eternal question, "Which came first, the chicken or the egg?"

Just as each Type has its own unique communication style, each of us has our own unique "conflict style" that correlates with our Enneagram Type. Again, the simple reason is that each Type is defined by our Core Motivations—Fear, Desire, Weakness, and Longing.

Conflict has occurred since the Fall of Man in Genesis 3 and until the Lord returns, we're going to continue to have conflict… simply because we live in a fallen world!

But under the guidance of the Holy Spirit, maybe we can do conflict "better" and actually use that conflict to draw us together rather than push us apart.

As a pastor, pastoral counselor, and mediator, I know that in desperation people will resort to just about any tactic to change someone's behavior—criticism, the silent treatment, or even "helpful suggestions"! Sadly, if it does have an impact it only changes the outward behaviors and never the heart. Usually, it just makes things worse.

The only thing that changes the heart of a person is the grace of Christ.

But how do we apply grace when we're in the midst of an emotional conflict—especially when it pops up when we're least expecting it?

For most of us, conflict is more about *perspective* differences rather than having the "right" answer. This means we are committing "assumicide" a ton in our marriages. Sadly, it's destroying us as individuals as well as our marriages. In other words, our "problem" is often not the problem. Our problem is actually how we see the problem and what we do with it. Our problem is our "perspective" of the problem, a perspective that comes out of our Core Motivations.

This was true for me.

I had been a pastor for quite some time when I began to realize that people were not responding to me in the ways I thought they would, especially Beth.

Today, most people would say I'm pretty calm and even-keeled… but a number of years ago as a young pastor and a young husband, internally I was more like a brewing storm rolling in to crash upon the shore.

My demeanor wasn't unpleasant, but I was sometimes sharp, abrupt, and almost waiting for someone to pick a fight. It was like I was testing people to see if they really cared about me, believing if they did, they would push back when I pushed forward (a typical Type 6 characteristic). But with Beth, "pushing back" wasn't even in her vocabulary as a Type 9, Peaceful Mediator.

Let's just say I wasn't getting the results I expected or wanted.

It was around this time I discovered Peacemaker Ministries. Here's how they define a Peacemaker:

"A peacemaker is a person that has chosen to engage in relational disputes with health and purpose from a Gospel perspective. They seek to work through healthy tension, rather than cause unhealthy conflict between them and others involved. They do this by reflecting on God's word, listening to others, considering other perspectives, taking responsibility for their actions, and committing to healthy reconciliation between them and the other person. Their goals are to deepen the relationship and to grow it through effective communication."

As a believer, I obviously, didn't want to repel or even distance people. I truly wanted to connect but something I was doing wasn't working… and I knew it was more *me* than them. Discovering Peacemaker Ministries (www.peacemaker.training) was the catalyst that sparked me wanting to work on myself and find a way to calm the inner storm that always seemed to be brewing in my soul.

In seminary, I had studied and dissected each word of James 4:1, "What causes fights and quarrels among you? Don't they come from your desires that battle within you?" But I realized I didn't know *how* to win the battle of those desires that were at war within my heart.

I began the Peacemaker training in 2005 and, for the next five years, I fully immersed myself in learning what I could do to become a peace *maker* instead of a peace *breaker*.

I took seriously the command in Matthew 7:5, "First take the log out of your own eye, and then you will see clearly to take the speck out of your brother's eye."

Learning about conflict and its resolution became my passion because of my own need, but I began to see that what I was learning could help others who were struggling in their own conflicts, which began my journey to become a certified conciliator and mediator.

It was around this same time that Beth immersed herself in finding out everything she could about the Enneagram and how it could apply to her heart.

As I was working on helping myself (and others) discover how to resolve conflict redemptively, I was perplexed that the tools I was using seemed more "general" and didn't take into account the uniqueness of each individual. And, at a much deeper level, I wanted to understand what was getting us into conflict in the first place. I know conflict is always going to be a part of life, but I didn't just want to "manage" conflict, I wanted to find ways to *use* conflict to become more Christlike in my relationships. (In theological terms, a process called sanctification.)

But as Beth has shared, until we learned through the tool of the Enneagram how our personality's unhealthy (and out of alignment with the Gospel) perceptions were negatively impacting our marriage, assumicide continued to wreak havoc in our relationship.

Gratefully, we discovered that when looking at each other through the lens of the Enneagram at our unique personality Types, we could choose to not believe the lies of our internal wiring that don't match up with what the Lord says of us. As we continued to learn more, we were able to accept that as a couple we fundamentally see the world from completely different perspectives and take those perspectives into consideration.

The truth is, for better or worse, the testing ground for all we were discovering was in our own relationship. And it wasn't (and isn't) always pretty!

Early on, it felt like we were trying to climb Mt. Everest with no equipment. We repeatedly would react hurtfully toward each other because something would activate or hurt us.

For most people, conflict happens when something activates us, and we respond lightning fast from somewhere deep within us. Often, we don't even know where it came from. In a brief moment, your thoughts, emotions, or gut are screaming at you to react.

Experience should tell us that it never works to react impulsively, but the pain, frustration, or hurt seems too much. So, we react. The side of us that is out of alignment with the Gospel (the less healthy part of our personality) urges us to respond in unhelpful (and often harmful) ways.

We often have the best of intentions not to "go there" but it just happens. Then your spouse responds in an all too familiar way and the next thing you know, you're back in the same rut, and it feels like you're trapped.

But there are four things we have learned to do (more accurately, we have trained our minds to do!) to combat "assumicide" and our natural reactiveness when a thought/feeling rushes in:

1. **Pause** and take it captive. (Pause and ask, "How am I seeing this situation from the perspective of my personality vs. the Gospel?")
2. **Pray** *immediately* and ask the Holy Spirit for patience and wisdom.
3. **Ask** clarifying questions of the other person. (How are they seeing the situation from the perspective of their personality?)
4. **Trust** in the truth of the Gospel.

Much of the time, the root of conflict comes from not truly knowing and understanding the heart of our spouse (and their motivations) and insisting that our point of view be seen as right. We believe *our* goals and interests are the right path.

The belief that "we are right, and they are wrong" keeps us in these same patterns of relating. It's like an old dance where we fall into the practiced steps of false thinking. This dance plays the same song of condemnation over and over again. We either condemn ourselves or our spouse. Our thoughts, feelings, assumptions, and reactions seem stuck. We can't seem to get out.

But there's a relatively simple reason we get caught in this dance and it's because our focus is off. If our focus is on "who's right and who's wrong" we are, indeed, stuck in the old pattern. But if our focus is on restoration, we can get free from the old dance steps we are in and enjoy a new dance where we're able to lean into each other and move with the music.

Here's an incredible fact about conflict that marriage researcher Dr. Gottman provides us: *69 percent of all conflicts have no right answer.*

Let me repeat that. Sixty-nine percent of our conflicts have no right answer.

Research shows that the *majority* of conflicts are because of personality differences and differing interpretations of life issues.

If 69 percent of all conflicts don't have a right answer, then why are we fighting?

Why do we end up isolating ourselves from one another and harming each other? What would it be like for us to participate in the truth of the Gospel where Christ is the one who is restoring each of us individually and as a couple?

The amazing news of the Gospel is that Christ is the one who is reconciling us to himself. He is, in fact, advocating for us right now before the throne of God. He is showing God that he removed our sin and placed his righteousness on us, which means that we are in a right relationship with God.

Christ is the one who is renewing us. Christ is the one who is redeeming us. Christ is the one who has restored us to a right relationship.

So, if Christ has restored us, how do we turn around and restore each other with the same love?

This is where we can make a choice to look at a situation we're in with our spouse, the person we love, from another perspective. A slight shift can make a world of difference.

Dr. Larry Crabb, in his book *Connecting*, said it this way, "A vision we give to others of who and what they could become has power when it echoes what the spirit has already spoken into their souls."

Just think about that for a moment. What if we not only try to see the situation from their perspective, but what if we look at *them* and who they are becoming from God's perspective?

When my heart is aligned with what God is doing in the life of my spouse, amazing and beautiful things can happen.

But the ironic thing is, most of the power to change the outcome of our conflicts happens *in the conflict!*

And that is a huge shift… from thinking about "us being right and them being wrong" to thinking, "What is God doing through them and in them and how can I help them become who he wants them to be?"

And to take it a step even further, what is God doing in *me* in this situation and what do I need to see differently?

Now don't miss what I'm saying… I'm not being a super spiritual Pollyanna and saying that if we just think positively about our spouse and how much God loves them in the midst of a conflict, it will all be instantly better, and we'll live happily ever after. Because that's not true.

What I am saying is that in the context of marriage, God changes each of us to become more like him… and he often uses our spouse to accomplish his purpose!

In his book *Marriage Rebranded*, Tyler Ward said, "Marriage, even though it will introduce us to some of life's most arduous moments, has brilliant intentions in mind. It's unapologetically interested in chipping away at our dysfunctional thoughts, patterns, and postures in life and inviting us—and our spouses—to become the best version of ourselves."

This means that when you are committing to growing and maturing in Christ, it is God's intention to use your spouse to further his purposes in your life.

Know this: God is using everything for our good and not to punish us.

So back to the question of how do we show grace to our spouse in the middle of a conflict? How can we join God in the process?

There are three fundamental elements that are essential:

First, trust the process.

It's God's desire and design to have your spouse in that intimate place in your life where they will see things other people may never see in you. God intends to use your spouse to bring these to light in order to gently restore you.

We do a lot of things to minimize our spouse's voice in our life (especially when we find them irritating or annoying!). We deny it. We escape from it. We make excuses. But if there's one invitation to those who silence their spouse, the Gospel invites us to accept their voice in your life and consider if it's the Father's intent to bring something to your attention.

Second, be open to blind spots.

Sin blinds. It deceives. Sadly, this is part of sin's deception and we buy into it all the time.

It may be uncomfortable, even initially hurtful, but your spouse may be picking up on something you are not aware of. It is important that you're open to what a loving and restorative spouse has to reflect back to you. (And if you don't feel your spouse is loving, that doesn't necessarily mean there's nothing for you to learn from the Lord even in difficult situations.) Seriously, there are things that I came to understand about who I am as a man, as a pastor, as a father, because my wife addressed it with me in a loving way even when it wasn't always pleasant to hear.

God says in James 1:2, "Count it all joy, my brothers, when you meet trials of various kinds…"

Welcome the feedback and remember that it's not just your spouse who's trying to help you, but it's the Father's purposes in using your spouse for your growth.

Third, growing is our responsibility in Christ.

Galatians 6:2 begins with the admonishment to "bear one another's burdens, and so fulfill the law of Christ" but Paul ends the paragraph in Galatians 6:5 with, "For each will have to bear his own load."

There is this tension in the text that seems to say that to love each other well, it's our personal responsibility to work on our own heart while also participating in God's work in the life of our spouse. Typical marriage arguments are, "If you wouldn't do this, I wouldn't do that." We think, "I only react that way because my spouse treats me in that way. If they would change, then I would stop."

But God points out to us that it's our responsibility to lift and carry our own load. Your spouse is not responsible for your growth. That is to be worked out between you and the Lord through his Holy Spirit who loves and cares for us and for our ultimate good.

Conflict is not something to be avoided, but rather the opportunity for us to experience the grace of God in a new way for the both of us, not just the one who has failed.

That said, what if your spouse isn't someone who seems committed to loving you and helping you grow in Christ and in your relationship? Is there a way to love them in a healthy way? Can you lovingly help them to become more aligned with the Gospel?

I believe the answer is yes and here's the reason why.

Dr. Paul Tripp says it well, "Marriage is meant to expose your self-focus and self-reliance. It is meant to convince you that you are needier than you thought you were and to encourage you that God's grace has more power to transform than you thought it did. Marriage is meant to teach you how to give, love, serve, forgive, support, encourage, and wait."

Now I understand there are peace *breakers* and there are peace *fakers*. (Let me reiterate, we're talking about normal, typical relationships, not spouses who are acutely dysfunctional or abusive.)

But here's what is important to remember for those who are delivering the truth of the Gospel to their spouse who has been caught in failure or sin.

Your spouse matters.

Your spouse is loved by the Lord with the exact same sacrificial love you are. Yes, if your spouse has made a mistake it may need to be addressed to further the Gospel in their life. Yes, if your spouse has a pattern or an incident of sin and failure in their life, they may need to have it reflected back to them *gently*. And yes, it is actually unkind and unloving for us to not to address issues with our spouse.

But for some of you, I ask that you put your weapon down. Even though we all do it to some degree, for some, you are super quick to bring up your spouse's mishaps, errors, wrongs, and sins. You feel it is your responsibility to fix your spouse and it is *not*. A quick and constant correction, or even "helpful suggestion," can easily be felt as condemnation.

In addition, there are those of us who avoid conflict at any cost. For us, our next challenging step is to engage, in love. Our neglect harms our marriages.

When we address our spouse with kindness and gentleness (and we are making an effort to understand how they view and perceive the world), they are more likely to receive our observations of the incident.

We have to check our own hearts *first*.

When our heart is in line with the truth of the Gospel, we will approach our spouse not with a heart that's agitated, wants revenge, or to punish, criticize or condemn but a heart that's full of the Spirit. And we will want to restore him or her in a spirit of gentleness—of soberness and kindness. Paul said in Romans 2:4, "God's kindness is meant to lead you to repentance."

Even if your spouse may not listen or get upset, remember, it's not your job to change them! That's the work of the Holy Spirit in them, just like it's the work of the Holy Spirit in you. If you are sharing with grace, truth, and love, you are simply participating in the life of Christ in your spouse's life.

In the end, you will have grown and so will your spouse.

In Ephesians 5, Paul says that "Christ loved the church and gave himself up for her, that he might sanctify her, having cleansed her by the washing of water with the word, so that he might present the church to himself in splendor, without spot or wrinkle or any such thing, that she might be holy and without blemish."

God is inviting us to participate in the work that he began by setting his love upon your spouse by pursuing them, by his Spirit, by calling them to himself, and now promising his work of growth in their life to present them in splendor and purity as a gift.

Tim Keller, in his book *The Meaning of Marriage,* says, "Within this Christian vision for marriage, here's what it means to fall in love. It is to look at another person and get a glimpse of the person God is creating, and to say, 'I see who God is making you, and it excites me! I want to be part of that. I want to partner with you and God in the journey you are taking to his throne. And when we get there, I will look at your magnificence and say, *I always knew you could be like this. I got glimpses of it on earth, but now look at you!*'"

Just think about that. What if your wife or husband turned to you, looked you in the eyes and said, "I am thrilled with what God is doing in your life; you are more beautiful to me now than ever."

Sound impossible? Remember, you can't strain infinite kindness. You can't tax eternal mercy. And you can't push God so hard that he decides you're not worth it.

Does redeeming conflict happen overnight? Of course not.

When we began this journey, Beth and I were out of shape and we stopped often and even slipped backwards at times. Graciously, the Lord took us each by the hand and walked with us step by step up the Mt. Everest we felt like we were climbing. He faithfully held on to us and guided us in his path.

We knew we were making progress, but we also knew we had a long way to go! This slow process of taking a few steps forward in grace but frequently sliding a few steps downward continued for years.

But over time, we began to see—and eventually value—our differences, and we realized a shift had happened.

One day not too long ago, it dawned on me that something amazing was happening: all those baby steps we had taken in learning how to communicate and understand one another were actually paying off.

You see, one evening I did something that earlier would have devastated Beth emotionally and shut her down completely. Yet, this time her response was different. (Remember, as a Type 9 she fundamentally believes that her presence doesn't matter.)

Beth and I were in the living room talking. She began to tell me about something that had happened and was including lots of detail (as she often does!). As she was telling me her story, I got up and went into the kitchen and started to crush ice for my 32 oz. Yeti cup. (And I'll admit our ice maker is loud, slow, and can be a bit annoying!)

As I started crushing the ice, (I found out later) Beth immediately felt crushed inside because her personality structure chimed in loudly, *Well, obviously he doesn't care what I have to say. My presence doesn't matter. My voice doesn't matter. If it did, he'd wait until I was done talking to get his ice.*

This internal reaction happened super-fast!

But here's the beautiful part. God made her aware of her "rumble strip." He helped her to instantly question her thought process. She'd learned to notice the lies and recognize them as lies (even though they felt true). It's like Pavlov's dog with an "awareness" bell. She noticed the thought as an alert to bring to mind what is true.

In the past, this could have turned into a huge issue. I would have been clueless, and Beth would have felt overlooked and unimportant to me even though that wasn't my intention. My action was having an impact even though I hadn't set out to make her feel like I wasn't paying attention to what she was saying, but my action had an impact nonetheless.

After a lot of practice, we've both trained our minds to ask ourselves clarifying questions to get back onto the path of truth and counter wrong thoughts. In this case, she said to herself, *Hold on a second. Is that true? Does Jeff really think my presence doesn't matter?*

By the time I was done crushing my ice and getting my drink, her thought process had shifted. *No. Jeff is my husband and best friend. He is listening to me, he's just getting ice. Everything is okay.*

It's vital that we see how extremely fast our Core Motivations can get activated!

We have to be ready (and trained) to steer our internal world back onto the path that is full of truth and healing.

As soon as I came back in and sat down, she began to laugh. She then told me what had gone on in her head. She was able to say to me, "Next time, would you mind saying, 'Hey, could you hold on a second? I want to hear what you have to say, but I need to get some ice.' That little shift would make such a difference to me."

Since we are both working on understanding how our internal world operates (and can share that with each other), we can show compassion and a desire to help each other and not take perceived affronts personally. For me, I didn't take her comments as criticism, since I'm aware of how her Type responds, so I didn't feel attacked. I was actually grateful for the feedback because I really do want to love her well, and I know she feels the same way about me. What in the past would have led to relational distance and conflict, this time led to connection, understanding, and growth.

Again, this is a learned process! It didn't happen overnight, and we are still working on using these "everyday challenges" as ways to learn to connect with each other and not pull back or attack each other.

My two takeaways:

1. I now routinely let her know I'm listening to her, especially when it may appear I'm not, since I know that's hard for her.
2. I bought a countertop ice maker that makes pellet "Sonic-style" ice but much more quietly!

As you can see, communication doesn't have to lead to conflicts and conflicts don't have to turn south. Instead, there can be harmony and restoration. This scenario easily could have turned into a conflict but because Beth was able to notice the rumble strip and talk about her thought process, we were able to resolve what could have led her to shut down and continue feeling hurt. I wouldn't have recognized it if she hadn't said something because I don't interpret life the same way she does.

If she did the exact same thing to me (crush ice in the middle of what I was saying), that action wouldn't have affected me in the least, because that's not what activates me.

The point is, start to become an observer. Notice when and why something bothers you. Look at what Core Motivations are activated inside you. How are you responding and why? What part of the Gospel did you forget and not trust in? How can you come back in alignment with the Gospel and trust in God to fulfill you?

Notice the healthy paths for your Type and, by faith, try them out knowing your Father will meet you there and help you. Relying on the guidance and strength of the Holy Spirit gives you the ability to change.

We know it's not easy, but the changes and steps toward becoming aligned with the Gospel often occur in daily decisions we make, not one massive, momentary effort. For Beth (and me), a step toward alignment happened in the time it takes to crush some ice.

That alignment can happen for you, too, if you set your heart every day in the direction of growth and the Gospel.

We all have a choice to make. We can be frustrated and angry when conflict happens, or we can trust the Holy Spirit to use conflict to help us grow in alignment with him.

Because, until the Lord comes again, there's going to be conflict!

But by his grace we can use conflict as a springboard to love one another and "so fulfill the law of Christ."

CHAPTER 8:

Becoming Our Best Selves

Jeff

Learning to communicate and resolve conflict with your spouse is a lot less about getting it right and more about gaining the emotional awareness to know what is happening in us and in them. What is keeping us from engaging intimately with each other and trusting God to take care of us in the process?

"Put on then, as God's chosen ones, holy and beloved, compassionate hearts, kindness, humility, meekness, and patience, bearing with one another and, if one has a complaint against another, forgiving each other; as the Lord has forgiven you, so you also must forgive. And above all these put on love, which binds everything together in perfect harmony. And let the peace of Christ rule in your hearts, to which indeed you were called in one body. And be thankful" (Col. 3:12–15).

But how do we begin to change habits that have been around for most of our lifetime?

First, be proactive on the positive. Focus on affirming your spouse in a multitude of ways, especially for who they are in Christ. Dr. Gottman has shown that **in order for a relationship to grow, you have to have *five* positives to *one* negative.**

Overtime, Dr. Gottman says, thriving marriages develop "Positive Sentiment Override," where both spouses begin to anticipate (or assume in a good way) a positive interaction or response from their spouse.

But if couples do not speak to their spouses positively in a five to one ratio, their relationship will develop "Negative Sentiment Override." In these situations, spouses will begin to assume and anticipate a negative response and then act on those assumptions as if they already occurred. This anticipation of a negative response leads to assumicide and the conversation is doomed to failure even before it begins.

For your relationship to thrive, it's essential that for every negative comment, judgment, or criticism, you find five positives to affirm. This means you have to look for positive things to affirm, and I can promise you that's easier to do when you're not in the middle of a conflict!

Second, he found that those with a thriving marriage "turn toward" their spouse's bids in a positive way 87 percent of the time. The marriages that were struggling turned toward their spouse's bids to connect [only] 33 percent of the time.

Simply put, *thriving* marriages seek out opportunities to connect with one another in more positive ways than negative.

When our hearts are at rest with the truth of the Gospel, we don't need to use demands, judgments, or punishments since Christ has perfectly satisfied our deepest need. This ultimately means we don't need for our spouse to come through for us like we thought or demanded—Christ already has! (We're not saying this is easy; we're just saying it's true.)

What this confirms is what we most likely already know… when we intentionally focus on the positive, we set ourselves up for a positive outcome.

But more importantly, when we turn toward our spouse in a positive and affirming manner, we are embodying the truth of the Gospel for them. We communicate to them that we see them, their needs, and that they are loved.

So, in the midst of a bid for connection (whether positive or negative), we can communicate that we see our spouse's need. We can demonstrate safety when they share, no matter how deep their needs are hidden under criticism, fear, or a demanding heart. And we can even move toward them by indicating we are there for them. We can do this since we can securely rely on the fact that the Gospel is at work within us.

Some great questions to ask ourselves:

- What fears pop up in my heart when thinking about sharing the deep longings of my heart?
- What might I be desiring more than connecting with my spouse?
- Am I willing to turn to Jesus with these fears and desires, and ask him to meet these needs so I can connect with my spouse on a deep and transformative way?

The other thing you can do is to be aware of "rumble strips" (our internal warning signals or alarms) when you are being activated. These signals can give you the option of responding in a more loving way.

When you're sensing the rumble strip warning, here is what Beth and I use as a simple focusing word when something is activating us.

We focus on becoming **A.W.A.R.E.** to grow in every area of life.

- **Awaken:** Notice how you are reacting in your behavior, feelings, thinking, and body sensations.
- **Welcome:** Be open to what you might learn and observe without condemnation and shame.
- **Ask:** Ask for the Holy Spirit to help clarify what is happening internally.
- **Receive:** Receive any insight and affirm your true identity as God's beloved child.
- **Enjoy:** Take comfort in being Christ's beloved child and enjoy your new freedom from old self-defeating patterns of living.

When our hearts have settled on Christ to meet *our* needs (and we aren't looking to our spouse for that fulfillment), we discover:

- We no longer need to be defensive about our needs or our mistakes, because Jesus has already made us holy in his work on the cross.
- We no longer have to prove ourselves as someone who deserves to be loved, because Jesus loves us completely.
- When we make mistakes, we are free to face our mistakes and failures honestly because Jesus has forgiven us.
- We can offer the same love, forgiveness, and peace to others that Jesus offers us.

Be Intentional about Affirmation

This is where the Enneagram can become extremely helpful in the hunt for the positives because this isn't always easy and takes practice (we know this from experience!). But you can start by looking to your spouse's Type to see what qualities you can purposely affirm.

For example, here are several things you can always affirm your spouse in for each Type.

- **Type 1:** They are ethical, reliable, productive, wise, idealistic, conscientious, orderly, and self-disciplined.
- **Type 2:** They are loving, caring, nurturing, compassionate, generous, supportive, and empathetic.
- **Type 3:** They are optimistic, motivating, efficient, excelling, accomplished, admirable, and organized.
- **Type 4:** They are compassionate, empathetic, introspective, supportive, creative, authentic, and emotionally deep.
- **Type 5:** They are objective, observant, perceptive, curious, analytical, thoughtful, and innovative.
- **Type 6:** They are loyal, committed, trustworthy, responsible, likable, compassionate, and hardworking.
- **Type 7:** They are fun-loving, imaginative, optimistic, enthusiastic, creative, quick, and joyous.
- **Type 8:** They are compassionate, protective, inspiring, resilient, empowering, self-assertive, and an advocate for the weak.
- **Type 9:** They are great listeners, thoughtful, kind, generous, patient, accepting, and peaceable.

Affirmation can seem awkward at first if it's not something you normally do. And as we said, it doesn't happen overnight.

Our friend, Kate, and her husband, Sam, were dating when they were in college. Kate had put on the "freshman fifteen" and was having a very hard time getting it off. She decided to go on a weight loss diet, which wasn't easy to do since she and Sam were on the college cafeteria meal plan (not to mention her love of the late-night chocolate chip cookie "study snacks" in the dorm). One day in frustration, she asked Sam for his help.

She said with glistening tears, "Oh Sam, I'm really struggling with my weight. My clothes are too tight, and I have to get this weight off. I'd love for you to help me stick to my diet. Would you?"

Sam (not knowing any better at the time) agreed.

They met up at the school cafeteria for lunch and went through the buffet line. Even though she only took a small helping, she couldn't resist the mashed potatoes that were served. Sam didn't say anything and after they got done eating, she said to him, "I can't believe I ate those mashed potatoes, but they were so good. Why didn't you say anything? I thought you said you were going to help me."

Sam said he was sorry, and they headed to class.

The next day they were going through the dinner line and as Kate reached for the serving spoon for the cherry cobbler, Sam said, "You know you really shouldn't eat that…"

Kate was furious! She said, "Sam, you're not the food police. I don't want you to tell me what I can and cannot eat!"

Sam wasn't sure what to do. This same scenario played out more than a few times!

Finally, one day, as they took their trays and sat down, Sam, with a distressed look on his face said to her, "Kate, I love you, but I need to know what you want me to do. If I don't say anything about what you're eating and you eat it, you get upset. If I say something about what you're eating, you get *more* upset! I'm confused and getting dumped on. Which is it?"

As soon as he said it, Kate saw that she had put Sam in a "no win" situation. She said to him, "Oh my gosh. I didn't realize I've been putting you in such a difficult position. You were really trying to help me, and I love that about you!"

They continued to eat and after a while she said to him, "Here's what I think might help... I know you can't win in this. Let's make a pact that from now on, my diet and what I eat, or don't eat, will be *totally* on me. I know you love me, and I won't ask you to be the food police. If I gain or if I lose, you won't be responsible. Does that work?"

Sam was visibly relieved and said that worked for him!

Since that time, Sam has been intentional about looking for positive things to affirm in Kate (that don't have to do with her weight!) and Kate has been committed to affirm him for the ways he is thoughtful toward others and the many ways he supports and cares for her.

They've now been married forty-three years (43!), they still affirm each other, and their pact is still holding!

Helping Our Spouse to Become Their Best Self

Beth

Helping our spouse to become *their* best self helps us to become *our* best self.

But here's a challenging statement...

> Helping our spouse to become their best self isn't about us changing them into who we think they should be; it's about coming alongside of them and loving them as they are becoming who God wants them to be.

Obviously, we can't just transform instantly into the perfect spouse just because we have some new knowledge. Trust me, if I could just immediately leave behind all of my problems and become the perfect spouse, I would have done so many years ago!

But the real power to become a loving spouse aligned with the Gospel comes when I surrender to the Holy Spirit and depend solely on him to do this transforming work inside *me*. When we struggle and want to grow, it allows us to walk with the Spirit and trust him in new and dynamic ways moment by moment, day by day.

Now, when Jeff sees that I'm super stressed and cranky, instead of committing "assumicide" and taking it personally, he can ask clarifying questions so he can better know how to help or understand me. He can have compassion and understanding for me instead of taking things out of context and overreacting. I can do the same for him.

This kind of awareness changes everything. It allows for forgiveness and real love to happen. It can change what could have been a hurtful fight or argument into a helpful exchange.

Additionally, we can also cheer each other on when we see growth happening. My path of growth might be an easy one for him, but when he sees how difficult it is for me, he can encourage me along the way. I can also do the same for him. This is exactly what Christ wants for us—to spur one another on to love and good deeds (Heb. 10:24).

The great news is simply this: The Holy Spirit is the one who is going to get us from our current location to our best destination, which is being more like Christ. And that's what makes a marriage, and all our relationships, thrive.

"Aha" Moments

I wish I had a nickel for every time someone said to me, "If only I had the Enneagram years ago! It could have saved so much trouble and heartache!"

Take our friends, Karen and Steve, for instance. Karen was excited to see her husband, Steve, after he had been gone on a long business trip. She was eager to connect with him and find out all about his trip, who he was with, where he'd gone to eat, the conversations he had experienced, etc. She was all about relationships, and she wanted him to feel loved and cared for by engaging with him about his time away.

When he would get home, she'd enthusiastically ask him questions, longing to reconnect over a conversation together after being apart for a week. But that is not what happened.

Typically, when he arrived home and walked in the door, he'd look at her blankly and wouldn't communicate with her much at all. In fact, he would give short, curt answers like, "I don't know. It went fine. I don't remember where we went to eat." Then he'd pick up the mail or walk away to change his clothes. She assumed he didn't want to communicate with her, which left her feeling devastated.

Every time this happened, she was crushed. She was hurt by his flat response and lack of reconnecting with her. She felt rejected and unwanted. Why wouldn't he talk with her? Why wouldn't he share what was going on in his life? Was she *that* unlovable?

But then, a few days later, he would casually mention that he went to this great steak house when he was on his business trip and continue to fill in some of the holes that he didn't communicate when he first arrived home. This turn of events really irritated her and she would think, *Well, why didn't you tell me that when I first asked?*

This particular hurtful "dance" continued between them for years. They were constantly stepping on each other's toes and hurting one another. He'd feel pressured and shut down, she'd try harder to connect, and they'd end up at odds. They couldn't understand how to fix it so they could actually dance together in an in-sync, beautiful way. Each of them tried to force the other to dance to their rhythm without understanding the other's rhythm, therefore, they could never get balanced with each other, which always perpetuated their relational tension.

When Karen became aware of the Enneagram, she began to realize how radically different his perspective and needs in life were than hers.

First, she learned that Steve was a Type 5, the Investigative Thinker. In learning more about him, she discovered that Type 5s have a limited amount of inner resources and relational energy and when that energy is depleted (usually from interacting with people), their tank is empty. They're totally spent, and they have *nothing* left to give. In fact, they fear being forced to continue to interact from this empty place since it feels like they will experience catastrophic depletion. This fear causes them to withdraw and isolate themselves so they can recharge.

It was helpful for her to learn that Type 5s are thinkers, not feelers, and they don't sense others' feelings and relationship needs easily. She also learned that she is a Type 2, the Supportive Advisor, who is all about relationally connecting with others through their feelings and meeting their needs. (As you can see, they are a great representation of the saying that opposites attract!)

After learning about his perspective and needs in life, Karen, at long last, had her "Aha!" moment. She finally understood that her husband's silence wasn't about him not wanting to connect with her *personally*. He was simply being true to his Type; when he came home from a highly interactive business trip, he was out of relationship energy. Understanding him more clearly allowed her to step back and give him the space he needed to restore his energy without her feelings being crushed or feeling rejected. She knew that in due time, his energy would be restored, and they could connect once again.

As she began to truly understand his world and love him in a way that resonated to him, he began to learn more about her as a Type 2. He realized that she needed some relational connection when he'd been gone for a while. He learned to say to her, "I'm spent right now and can't offer much from my end, but I'm happy to sit here with you and hear about your day and what's been going on with you."

This slight but momentous shift in their relationship enabled her to feel heard by him, which left her feeling loved and wanted… *her Core Desire* (and he was happy because he didn't have to use many words!).

The Enneagram brings these amazing "Aha" moments into our lives and relationships so we can better understand one another. This deeper understanding creates more compassion, care, empathy, grace, mercy, forgiveness, and reconciliation.

Becoming Us is all about the *process* of understanding your own heart's motivations and learning how to better communicate with one another through the lens of the Enneagram. You can have a relationship where you love each other well and point one another back to Christ, who truly meets our deepest needs.

The fun part is that you get to learn and connect with your spouse in new and meaningful ways. You may find yourself being surprised, thinking, "Oh, that's why he (or she) always does that!"

Using the Enneagram helps you transform into an objective observer looking from the outside in instead of being simply a participant in the situation. It gives you a new perspective, a common language, and profound understanding. Gaining these new insights can help each of you to avoid hurtful interactions and replace them with honesty, empathy, and deeper connection between you both.

Yes, this process of getting to know yourself and your spouse in more profound ways will be challenging. But with understanding, compassion, and practice, it enables you to truly know your needs and your spouse's needs, which are always satisfied in Christ.

With practice, you will learn how to graciously point yourself back to Christ to get replenished, which has the added benefit of letting your spouse see how they can get replenished in Christ, too.

Not only that, but the process of *Becoming Us* will help you to know how to relate to your spouse in ways that actually allow you to get your needs met while meeting the needs of the spouse you love. You, too, can have your own insightful "aha" moments.

Your Kitchen Table

As we gather around our well-worn kitchen table, we are so grateful it has become a secure, safe place where we can sit and communicate with each other, our family, our friends, and our clients (oh yeah, and have some great meals, too!).

Long ago on that cold, gray day when our friends John and Emily came to meet with us, it felt to them like a winter chill was in the air. But as cliché as it may sound, spring really was coming. And like spring, things didn't change overnight. Gradually, some shoots began to emerge, and they began to see some progress they hadn't seen before—not because of us *per se* but because they were committed to growing in Christ and looking for a way to break out of the hard season they were in. (They had been feeling like it was, "Always winter but never Christmas," for you *The Lion, The Witch and the Wardrobe* fans).

As Emily and John each explored their Core Motivations through the Enneagram, they saw their need for Jesus and found hope in him. They also gained new tools that led them back to Jesus and each other when their hearts were tempted to fall into old, defeating patterns.

So, if things are hard in your marriage, take heart, there is hope. It may take a while for a "thaw" to begin. But it *can* begin. If your marriage could use some "spring cleaning," that can happen, too. It's never too late to learn to love each other better.

Jeff and I would love to be invited to join you at your "kitchen table" and come alongside you with some of the lessons we have gleaned from using the Enneagram to help our relationship. Obviously, your table doesn't look like ours, but it can represent a place where you can sit and talk with open eyes and open hearts and be able to look at each other through the different lenses of the Enneagram.

That's the point, really… to communicate with each other and love each other well, to resolve conflict (maybe even a little more quickly), to respect and honor one another for what we each uniquely bring to the table… and give grace and mercy to each other as we grow in understanding and love in Christ.

Becoming the New Me
Our Hope for You—Gospel Transformation

Beth

Jeff and I know growth is *not* easy. In fact, it can be incredibly hard. It requires us to surrender unto the Holy Spirit, depend on him, and walk in accordance to his calling for us. But when we let go of our control and he takes over, our thirst will be quenched, and his blessings will flow into our lives and marriages.

In our experience, as Gospel transformation takes place, the ripple effects will not only have a positive effect in your own life but also have a positive impact on all those you encounter… like when you throw a rock into a pond and you can see the circles starting small and getting larger as they go farther and farther out.

As I began to transform and become more aligned with the Gospel (and make no mistake, I'm *still* in progress!), the changes I was making helped transform my relationship with Jeff and the people around me. As Jeff began to transform and become more aligned with the Gospel, the same thing happened to him (not at the same time, but eventually we began to see each other through the other's lens). The process started with small ripples, and then spread out in increasing circles, first to each other, but then to others.

Those increasing circles meant more and more friends, acquaintances, and even strangers were experiencing the transformation that comes from the Gospel through the tool of the Enneagram. I never would have dreamed that God would use our bumpy marriage journey and personal stories of transformation to encourage others, but in the context of marriage, we are all alike, striving to love each other and more fully understand who we are in Christ—his beloved child.

Jeff and I can't wait to look down the road a year from now, five years from now, or even a decade from now, and see the ripple effects that your transformation has created for hope, wholeness, and freedom for yourself and for others.

That's why what excites us now is to think about YOU!

What is God going to do in you with this new understanding of yourself and your spouse? What are the things you'll hear the Lord whisper in your heart that will begin to set you free? And as you are transformed by the Gospel, how will that change transform the other people in your life?

Here's our greatest desire...

First, that you will know, believe, and trust in your identity in Christ. In Christ, you are completely forgiven and set free, and you have his complete righteousness on you and in you. When God looks at you, he is satisfied by Christ's finished work. And because of Christ's finished work on your behalf, he looks at you and sees his most cherished and beloved child. This knowledge and unconditional love will radically change everything in you—it is the ultimate transformation from death to life. (To God be the glory!)

Second, that as you find your Enneagram Type, you'll recognize how a personality apart from Christ is running *away* from its

Core Fear, running *toward* its Core Desire, *stumbling* over its Core Weakness, and *desperate* to hear its Core Longing.

As you become aware of these traits, you can make them the "rumble strip" alarms to make you aware of what's going on in your heart. You can ask the Holy Spirit to help you navigate your internal world. These "rumble strips" will refocus you toward being aligned with the Gospel, traveling the best path for your heart and personality Type.

Third, that God will reveal to you, both in knowledge and in experience, the transformative work of the Holy Spirit. As you become fully aligned with the Gospel, you can move toward growth, using all the various tools of the Enneagram (Wings, Arrows, Triads, Levels of Alignment, etc.) to bring out the very best in you, the way God designed you to be. When you are in this place of being fully aligned with Christ, others will be blessed, God will be glorified, and you will experience the closeness of a Savior who will always meet your every longing and need.

Our prayer for you is simply this:

May the Gospel meet you where you are, draw you closer to God and each other, and with open arms may you embrace this great, hope-filled destination, *Becoming Us*.

PART 2

How to Use the Enneagram Roadmap

Just as a GPS will give us directions like, "Approaching right turn," or "Proceed to the highlighted route," we have created an Enneagram Roadmap for you and your spouse.

The Enneagram Roadmap will list each of the nine Types in two parts:

The first part is called "Understanding Me" and the second part is called "Understanding Them."

Here's an example of how you can use the Roadmap.

If you're a Type 3, go to the "Type 3" section and read "Understanding Me."

Then, if your spouse wants to know about you and understand you better, they can go to the "Type 3" and read "Understanding Them."

The same is true for all the Types, so any combination of Types will work!

And if you're two of the same Types married to each other, it still works since you will be using different parts (Wings, Arrows, Levels of Alignment, and more) differently.

Obviously, *all* the information in each section is appropriate for understanding each Type, and we have put it into an easy format so you can use it like a GPS guide as you journey down the road as a couple. Remember, every element in the Enneagram Roadmap has been discussed previously, so you can always refer back to those elements for further clarification.

You'll find a variety of subjects about each Type:

In "Understanding Me," you'll find...
- A summary of each Type
- Primary perspective
- Core motivations
- Childhood patterns
- Wings
- Stress and growth paths
- Levels of alignment with the Gospel
- Communication style
- Conflict style
- Gospel transformation

In "Understanding Them," you'll find...
- Helpful insight to understand them as their Type
- Recognize behavior tendencies when their Type is activated
- Ways to improve communication with your spouse's Type
- How to relate to their Type in conflict
- When your spouse's Type is at their best
- Affirming your spouse's Type
- How to love your spouse (Type) better

Remember, the more you know about yourself, the more your spouse knows about themselves, and the more you know about each other, the easier it is to "recalibrate" when going off track and stay on course for your destination: a thriving and Gospel-centered marriage.

We hope you find the Enneagram Roadmap a helpful guide and enjoy the adventure of *Becoming Us*!

TYPE 1

Type 1: The Moral Perfectionist

Conscientious | Orderly | Appropriate | Ethical | Judgmental

Understanding Me

Summary of Type 1: The Moral Perfectionist is conscientious, orderly, appropriate, ethical, judgmental.

You walk through life seeing the way things should be and always striving to do what is right, wanting to be responsible and improve everything around you.

However, the world is imperfect and you can't escape feeling like these imperfections are assaulting you wherever you turn. You feel compelled to take on a personal obligation to improve these errors in the world. This overwhelming burden leaves you with chronic dissatisfaction, as the work of improving things is never finished.

You will never say you're angry because that would be "bad," and your deep desire is to be seen as "good." But you wrestle with resentment because you can't control life and make everything right.

When trying to satisfy your longing for things to be "good and right" apart from Christ, you can become perfectionistic and controlling, both of yourself and others.

Internally, you struggle to believe you are good or worthy because of the inner critic that constantly finds fault with everything you do. To silence this berating voice, you are extremely hard on yourself, striving to never make mistakes, which is exhausting.

You also struggle in relationships when others interpret your "helpful advice" as criticism and judgment or perceive you as overly demanding of perfection, even though your heart truly longs to help.

However, when your heart is aligned with the gospel and you learn to take your longings to Christ, you are able to let go of the unrealistically high standards you hold. As you rest in Christ, you no longer have to prove you are worthy or that you need to earn the love you so desperately long to receive. Your principled and purposeful nature can then bring out the best in yourself and others, truly making the world a better place.

Primary Perspective

- You believe you must fix and improve the world because it is full of imperfections.
- Your primary focus of attention is seeing errors, mistakes, and problems that need fixing. You are not seeking imperfections; they leap out at you and virtually assault you.
- You believe everything can and should be done in a right, perfect, orderly, and systematic way. You follow particular procedures to complete each task with precision and accuracy.

Core Motivations

Core Fear: Being wrong, bad, evil, inappropriate, unredeemable, or corruptible.
Core Desire: Having integrity, being good, ethical, balanced, accurate, virtuous, and right.

Core Weakness: *Resentment—*Repressing anger that leads to continual frustration and dissatisfaction with yourself, others, and the world for not being perfect.
Core Longing: "You are good."

Childhood Patterns

Childhood Message: "It is not okay to be wrong or make mistakes."

Message Your Heart Longs to Hear (Core Longing): "You are good."

The Type 1 as a Child

Your inner critic felt that the authority over you did not give you sufficient rules, so it created more rigorous rules for you to follow. You made every effort not to be wrong or bad and to avoid condemnation and punishment by striving for perfection in obeying all the rules. It was (and remains) exhausting to try to please your inner critic, who is constantly berating you. Your current resentment is actually deep sorrow for thinking you had to be the responsible adult instead of a playful child.

Wings

Type 1 Wing 9 (1w9)
"The Idealist"

- **In General:** Analytical, withdrawn, and detached from your emotions. Gentler, softer, calmer, quieter, and more generous.
- **When Struggling:** Stiffer, more subdued and impatient, speaking down to others from a distant and judgmental stance.
- **Both Types Are in Conflict with Each Other:** Type 9 is trying to avoid stirring up tension, while Type 1 provokes others to improve and do what is right.
- **Inspiring Quality:** Making others aware of society's needs by seeing what is wrong (Type 1) and expressing it in ways that are easier for people to receive (Type 9).

Type 1 Wing 2 (1w2)
"The Advocate"

- **In General:** Relationally warmer than 1w9, helpful, critical, vocal, social, controlling, and action-oriented.
- **When Struggling:** More rigid and intrusive (crossing relational boundaries) with your advice, insisting others follow your precise advice to change.
- **Both Types Blend Easily with Each Other:** Both types support each other in distinct ways—the Type 1 in being good and the Type 2 in being loving.
- **Inspiring Quality:** Seeing what is wrong and broken but rolling up your sleeves to help fix the problem instead of criticizing from a distance, like the 1w9.

Stress and Growth Paths

Stress | Type 1 moves toward Average to Unhealthy Type 4

- You feel resentful and indignant that others are not fulfilling expectations.
- The anger you have pushed down has turned into depression.

Growth | Type 1 moves toward Healthy side of Type 7

- You experience grace and joy, which creates a more self-accepting heart.
- You become more enthusiastic, spontaneous, joyful, positive, and optimistic, enjoying life more.

Levels of Alignment with the Gospel

Aligned (Living as His Beloved)
- Serving the world and others with patience and integrity.
- Realizing you're fully loved and accepted based on Christ's perfect work on your behalf.
- Trusting in Christ's forgiveness and righteousness to enable you to be more compassionate and gracious to yourself and others because you no longer need to strive for perfection to be loved and accepted.
- Believing there is no more condemnation in Christ, you're able to forgive yourself and others and demonstrate Christlike patience while remaining principled and responsible.

Misaligned (Living in Our Own Strength)
- Listening to your inner critic constantly pointing out your mistakes and demanding you fix any imperfections.
- Obeying your inner critic, which constantly hounds you to perfect yourself, others, and the world.
- Tirelessly pursuing perfection in all areas in hopes that your inner critic will finally quiet down and stop constantly berating you.
- Living in bondage to your inner critic, because the more you try to appease it by striving for perfection, the more you see mistakes and imperfections.

Out of Alignment (Living as an Orphan)
- Fixating on the smallest imperfections in yourself, others, and the world.
- Obsessing over micromanaging and asserting your control on everyone and everything in an effort to gain relief from the tyranny of your inner critic.
- Hurting your relationships with others and yourself when these efforts to perfect everything unfortunately only compound your problems.

Instead of living in bondage to perfection, surrender to the Holy Spirit, and depend on him completely. He will align you with the gospel, which is where you'll find true freedom and rest.

Communication Style
Teaching | Mentoring | Preaching | Reforming

Your Communication Tendencies

When you are doing well, you are honest, fair, poised, polite, and sincere. Your ideas and opinions are sound and reasonable, and you make sure goodness prevails for everyone.

When you are NOT doing well, you can speak in a teaching, correcting, and judgmental way, becoming easily irritated and opinionated, showing your displeasure visibly and through criticism.

Growth Areas for a Type 1's Communication Style
- Affirm and encourage, showing more warmth, compassion, and flexibility.
- Avoid picking on small details with your insights or criticisms.
- Remind yourself that it is God's responsibility to change or perfect others or the world, not yours.
- Put your full trust in God's care and timing, becoming more patient, forgiving, and gracious.

Conflict Style

Common Conflict Activators
- Being criticized or scrutinized
- Seeing people being deceptive, irresponsible, and lazy
- Knowing people are not taking responsibility or failing to complete their responsibilities with precision and accuracy

Growth Areas for a Type 1's Conflict Style
- Extend grace, mercy, compassion, and forgiveness to others.
- Trust the Holy Spirit to do his work in you and in others in his time.
- Ask clarifying questions instead of making judgment statements.
- Assume people are trying their best in life.
- Offer affirmation and encouragement instead of criticism or condemnation.

Gospel Transformation

Christ Satisfies Your Core Longing

You long to hear, "You are good," yet no matter how much people try, no one can fully satisfy this longing. But Christ did and did so specifically for you as a Type 1 in these ways:

1. **You are forgiven:** Jesus' death on the cross fully paid for all your sins—past, present, and future.

2. **His righteousness is credited to you:** Not only has Christ forgiven your debt, but he has also satisfied your need for righteousness. God has declared you righteous, not because of your perfections, but because he has credited Christ's perfect righteousness to you. Therefore, when God looks at you now, he only sees Christ's righteousness.

Growth Path for the Type 1

- Discern the difference between your inner critic and the Holy Spirit. Your inner critic condemns, berates, shames, judges, and punishes. The Holy Spirit forgives and frees you, granting righteousness, love, kindness, gentleness, patience, mercy, grace, and unconditional love.
- Trust in Christ's righteousness by treating yourself gently when you make a mistake. Using Romans 8:1, "There is now no condemnation for those in Christ Jesus," ask the Holy Spirit to quiet your inner critic so you can hear Christ's affirmations and assurances.
- Extend the same grace, compassion, and forgiveness to yourself and others that God has shown to you.
- Rest in God's sovereign care by giving him your irritations and trusting him with perfecting the world, others, and yourself.
- Trust that Christ is restoring all things, let go of being "the Adult," and embrace childlike joy.

Understanding Them

Helpful Insight to Understand a Type 1

A very loud, constant, and mean inner critic has constantly been berating, correcting, and controlling Ones their whole lives. Ones continually try to appease this ruthless inner critic by perfectly living up to its extraordinarily high standards, hoping for some reprieve from its constant onslaught of criticism. This is why Ones become irritated when others do not strive for the same level of perfection. And because Ones are already full of criticisms from this inner critic, they can become extremely hurt and defensive, criticizing others when others bring accusations against them.

Recognize Behavior Tendencies When a Type 1 is Activated

An activated Type 1 can:
- Speak in a sharp, curt manner with detailed judgments and criticisms.
- Bring up accusations related to other issues.
- Become rigid and inflexible on standards, seeming self-righteous.
- Show their inner anger through nonverbal cues (pursed lips, tight jaw, glaring eyes, tense upper body).

Ways to Improve Communication with a Type 1 Spouse

- Realize Ones are not searching for imperfections; mistakes assault them.
- Demonstrate empathy for how greatly they suffer under their spiteful inner critic.
- Ask how you can help relieve the burdens of their inner critic.
- Don't commit "assumicide"—thinking your Type 1 is just judging you. Instead, see how the One is trying to help with their "advice."
- Provide constructive, purposeful, and thoughtful conversations to solve issues.
- Affirm and support the One genuinely based on facts, not just feelings.
- Inform the One of your needs without accusing or criticizing.
- Repeat what the One said, asking clarifying questions to verify that you're on the same page.

How to Relate to a Type 1 in Conflict

- Take a problem-solving approach.
- Keep the conversation productive instead of demanding emotional responses.

- Discuss issues reasonably, relying on wisdom, insights, and facts.
- Provide structure to the conversation.
- Listen to the One's thoughts, criticisms, and judgments without assuming an intention to hurt you.
- Discuss the issues and facts at hand, avoiding personal criticism and attacks when you're ready to respond.
- Demonstrate your awareness of the inner critic's never-ending list by being gentle, kind, gracious, and a good listener.

Type 1s Are at Their Best When They:
- Show wisdom, balance, kindness, and respect.
- Find the most compassionate and appropriate action.
- Display nobility, peace, and gracious empathy.
- Serve the world and others with patience and integrity.
- Stop striving for perfection to gain love and acceptance.
- Rest fully in the forgiveness and righteousness they have in Christ.
- Demonstrate Christlike patience while remaining principled and responsible.

Affirm Your Type 1 Spouse When They:
- Surrender their resentment and trust in God's timing and care.
- Show gratitude and serenity.
- Express compassion instead of judgment.
- Trust in Christ's righteousness, not their loud inner critic.
- Embrace "good enough" over perfection.

How to Love Your Type 1 Better
- Take your own responsibilities seriously.
- Point out how good, responsible, and thorough they are.
- Understand their criticism as a sign that their inner critic is torturing them and remind them, "You are good because of Christ in you."
- Ask for forgiveness quickly when you're wrong, enabling a faster reconciliation.
- Remind them often of your love and Christ's love.
- Point to God's grace, which erases shame and enables them to be freer and more childlike.
- Praise God for the work he is doing in and through your Type 1 spouse when you see them living in alignment with the gospel.

Type 2: The Supportive Advisor

Thoughtful | Generous | Demonstrative | People-Pleasing | Possessive

Understanding Me

Summary of Type 2: The Supportive Advisor is thoughtful, generous, demonstrative, people-pleasing, possessive.

You see the world through relationships, believing that all people deserve to feel that someone loves and cares for them. You take a genuine interest in others and support anyone in need through your acts of service, helpful advice, and nurturing disposition.

Because of your natural sensitivity and empathy to the needs of people who are hurting, you intuitively know how to help. You feel responsible to provide support and attend to needs whenever you encounter them. However, the immense depth of need and suffering in our world can often leave you running endlessly, with no time to take care of yourself.

Being a helper satisfies you because, deep down, you struggle to believe that the people in your life love and want you apart from the help and support you offer. In your attempt to satisfy this longing to be loved and appreciated apart from Christ, you can become people-pleasing and possessive, inserting yourself into the lives of others, ignoring boundaries, and self-centeredly finding ways to be needed.

This overwhelming burden to care for everyone else damages you when you begin to attend to others' needs without adequately dealing with your own. In your pride, you can believe you know what's best for everyone else, while being in denial about the extent of your own needs, insisting that your only concern is taking care of others.

Relationally, you can struggle when others feel crowded by your efforts to help. You may feel hurt and insecure when you aren't needed, so you try to redouble your efforts to win people over by looking for things to do and say that will make people like and depend on you.

However, when your heart is aligned with the gospel and you learn to take your longings to Christ, you begin to take care of yourself and your own needs, knowing you are wanted and loved apart from what you can do for others. From that place flows selfless generosity and encouragement, a redemptive source of kindness and love in our world.

Primary Perspective

- You don't believe others love you unconditionally simply for who you are; you feel you must win the approval of others by feeling their emotions and fulfilling their needs.
- You project the image of being a completely selfless, loving, and supportive person in order to earn the approval and affirmation of others.
- You are convinced others will consider your recognizing and taking care of your own needs (emotional, relational, or physical) as "selfish" and reject you.
- You hide your needs from yourself and others and focus strictly on others' needs.

Core Motivations

Core Fear: Being rejected and unwanted, being thought worthless, needy, inconsequential, dispensable, or unworthy of love.

Core Desire: Being appreciated, loved, and wanted.

Core Weakness: *Pride—* Denying your own needs and emotions while using your intuition to discover and focus on the emotions and needs of others, confidently inserting your helpful support in hopes that others will say how grateful they are for your thoughtful care.

Core Longing: "You are wanted and loved."

Childhood Patterns

Childhood Message: "It's not okay to have needs of your own."

Message Your Heart Longs to Hear (Core Longing):
"You are wanted and loved. You don't have to give to earn my love."

Type 2 as a Child

You feared being rejected, unwanted, and unloved, so you became a "little helper" who selflessly loved and cared for others to gain their love, appreciation, and approval. After being "helpful," you would constantly measure their responses to assess if you'd earned the love and approval you believed you needed. If you didn't receive it, you might have become more intrusive with your "helpful" strategies to get the responses you craved.

Wings

Type 2 Wing 1 (2w1)
"The Servant"

- **In General:** Objective and serious with more self-control of your emotions and a drive to help others see what is right and good, a strong sense of responsibility to do what is right for others. Quietly serves behind the scenes.
- **When Struggling:** More insistent, controlling, and impatient, demanding others follow your moral advice.
- **Both Types Are in Conflict with Each Other:** Struggles more with self-condemnation and guilt than the Type 2w3.
- **Inspiring Quality:** Excellent teachers who focus on improving the lives of others through care and nurture by combining principles, values, encouragement, and relational warmth.

Type 2 Wing 3 (2w3)
"The Host/Hostess"

- **In General:** Outgoing, affirming, sociable, and self-assured; blesses others more overtly with your many talents. Wants the reputation of being desirable and likable and focuses more on succeeding relationally and professionally.
- **When Struggling:** Overly focused on winning approval, affirmation, and praise from others through flattery and charm.
- **Both Types Blend Easily with Each Other:** Both types are personable, charming, and adaptable, desiring to be liked and valued.
- **Inspiring Quality:** A very likable, charming, and outgoing person who enjoys and thrives in the spotlight.

Stress and Growth Paths

Stress | Type 2 moves toward Average to Unhealthy Type 8

- You suddenly become irritable, defensive, controlling, aggressive, demanding, and dominating.
- You'll blame others for problems while seeing your intentions as only good.

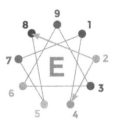

Growth | Type 2 moves toward Healthy side of Type 4

- You become more nurturing and compassionate toward yourself.
- You're more aware of your emotions, beginning to admit and accept painful feelings like anger, sadness, and loneliness.

Levels of Alignment with the Gospel

TYPE 2

Aligned (Living as His Beloved)
- Loving, caring, and supporting yourself and others selflessly without constantly needing love and affection from others.
- Knowing that Christ is caring for your emotional, relational, and physical needs now and from now on.
- Recognizing your own needs and asking for help.
- Maintaining appropriate boundaries by saying "no" when helping or caring for someone is not your responsibility.
- Allowing helpfulness to overflow from enjoying Christ's love and appreciation, not from needing the approval or appreciation of others.

Misaligned (Living in Our Own Strength)
- Believing you have to earn love and affection by helping, supporting, and advising others.
- Creating dependencies so you'll be needed.
- Hiding your own needs and emotions in fear that they'll threaten your relationships and keep others from giving you appreciation and love.
- Taking offense when others don't help and support you in the same way you love and support them, reinforcing your belief that you're not loved or wanted.
- Assuming that all your intentions and motives come from a good place in your heart with no hidden agendas.

Out of Alignment (Living as an Orphan)
- Believing your worth completely depends on affirmations and appreciation.
- Failing to see your need for help, rest, and renewal.
- Allowing your constant need to be needed and insistence that others receive your help (even when they didn't want or ask for it) to cause you exhaustion and illness.
- Manipulating others and acting like a martyr to convince them you're the ultimate giver and that your motives are pure and good.
- Getting passive-aggressive or just aggressive when others don't appreciate your help.

Instead of living in bondage to need, surrender to the Holy Spirit and depend on him completely, and he will align you with the gospel, where you'll find true freedom and rest.

TYPE 2

Encourager | Advice-Giver | Flatterer | Comforter

Your Communication Tendencies

When you are doing well, you ask good questions and give helpful guidance; you're an empathetic listener and a warm, compassionate presence.

When you are NOT doing well, you're either passive-aggressive and irritable or demanding and direct, giving unsolicited advice. When you have overextended yourself by helping others, you can channel your hurt and anger into manipulating and complaining.

Growth Areas for a Type 2's Communication Style
- Learn when you're too direct, demanding, irritable, passive-aggressive, manipulative, or complaining. This can be challenging since you typically only see your motives as pure.
- Express your feelings and needs to others so you can bless others and yourself from a heart that is rested and refreshed.
- Ask if the person who you feel needs your support, care, and advice wants to receive it, then maintain healthy boundaries.

Conflict Style

Common Conflict Activators
- Being taken for granted
- Feeling unappreciated or under appreciated
- Not feeling heard by others
- Sensing you're not needed or wanted
- Feeling rejected or dispensable

Growth Areas for a Type 2's Conflict Style
- Ask great questions that help others guide themselves toward good solutions instead of quickly inserting your advice.
- Acknowledge that your overly confident advice-giving can contribute to tension.
- Remain patient rather than telling everyone what they need to do.
- Remind yourself that Christ loves and wants you, and you no longer depend on others' approval, gratitude, and encouragement.

Gospel Transformation

Christ Satisfies Your Core Longing
You long to hear, "You are wanted and loved unconditionally," yet no matter how much people try to satisfy this longing, they cannot. But Christ did and did so specifically for you as a Type 2 in these ways:

1. **You are wanted:** Jesus pursued you, enduring difficulties and dying a painful death, because he wanted YOU. You are so valuable to him that he laid his own life down for you.

2. **You are loved:** Jesus demonstrated the ultimate act of love, care, and support by sacrificing himself for you. You had a great need because of your sin, and he perfectly took care of this need so you can have his righteousness and be forgiven.

Growth Path for the Type 2
- Realize Christ had needs and he took care of himself. Was he selfish? Nope! He is our perfect example of balancing self-care and loving others well.
- Acknowledge your needs. Do not hide them. Take actionable steps to provide yourself with great nurture so you can bless others with a renewed self.
- When you feel the need to earn love and approval, remind yourself who you really are: Christ's beloved and cherished child whom he pursued and brought close to himself because he loves you.
- Before helping someone, ask yourself if this circumstance is your responsibility. Is it time for you to trust God to provide outside of you?
- Memorize scriptures that remind you of the truth that Christ loves and wants you, regardless of what you do to help others.

Understanding Them

Helpful Insight to Understand a Type 2

Type 2's inner voice tells them they are being selfish and don't deserve to be loved and wanted if they ever focus on themselves and not others. Being rejected, unwanted, and unloved is their greatest fear, so they believe they must focus on others' feelings, needs, and emotions.

Because Twos intuitively know people's needs and emotions, they confidently insert their help, advice, and encouragement, hoping others will express their thankfulness and amazement at their kindness and help. Without this acknowledgment, hurting Twos will start to use manipulation, flattery, and people-pleasing to force others to express the appreciation and approval the Two feels they need.

Recognize Behavior Tendencies When a Type 2 is Activated

An activated Type 2 can:
- Withhold feelings from others.
- Express emotions intensely.
- Extensively express how they feel, why they feel that way, and what they believe others did wrong.
- Become either passive-aggressive and manipulative or aggressive, demanding, and controlling.

Ways to Improve Communication with a Type 2 Spouse

- Make sure you are warm, affectionate, and relationally connected with the Two before addressing any feedback. Use positive energy and an encouraging tone.
- Use the "sandwich method" (say something affirming, then gently tell them what you need to say, and follow with more affirmation) when you need to tell them something that might hurt or discourage them so their heart can be more receptive and less defensive.
- Discuss anything challenging or difficult privately; speaking in front of others causes the Two to feel a great deal of shame and rejection.
- Reinforce your feelings of love and support for the Two when finishing your discussion.
- Affirm that your love and care are unconditional and not determined or swayed by circumstances.

How to Relate to a Type 2 in Conflict
- Be patient and receptive, allowing them to talk extensively and process externally.
- Paraphrase what they said to make sure you heard them accurately. If you did not hear them right, ask clarifying questions and show them you want to understand them.
- Make every effort not to use accusatory words or body language that can shame, hurt, and close off the highly sensitive Two.
- Take the time to focus on their thoughts and feelings with curiosity and follow with encouragement or affirmation.

Type 2s Are at Their Best When They:
- Are sincere, humble, altruistic, warm-hearted, caring, and generous.
- Give unconditional love to themselves and others.
- Interpret the behavior of others charitably, emphasizing the good in people.
- Maintain a generous approach to life because they're taking care of their own needs.
- Give without strings attached.
- Maintain appropriate relationship boundaries by saying "no" to what is not their responsibility and not inserting their help when it is not wanted.

Affirm Your Type 2 Spouse When They:
- Show kindness to themselves by caring for themselves like Christ did for himself.
- Point others to Christ instead of needing others to depend on them.
- Base their value on being Christ's beloved child instead of on others' appreciation.

How to Love Your Type 2 Better
- Demonstrate your love by telling them specifically what you appreciate about them.
- Take the time to ask about their life, feelings, and needs, and be patient as they answer. Though they may deflect back to you, do not take the bait; keep the focus on them.
- Surprise them with creative gifts or time together, as they're always surprising others.
- Remove any hindrances from the Two's life so they can take care of themselves.
- Encourage them to draw on Christ's love and affirmation instead of trying to earn approval from others.

Type 3: The Successful Achiever

Efficient | Accomplished | Motivating | Driven | Image-Conscious

Understanding Me

Summary of Type 3: The Successful Achiever is efficient, accomplished, motivating, driven, image-conscious.

You are an optimistic, accomplished, and adaptable person who is able to see all that can be achieved in life. You always excel and are able to reach ambitious goals with apparent ease and confidence.

However, in our fast-paced and comparison-driven society, there are limitless opportunities for you to achieve more, drive results, and succeed in new ways. You struggle with the belief that you must excel at everything. Burdened to appear confident, successful, and impressive, you live under constant pressure to measure your worth by external achievement and a successful image.

Your deep fear of failure, or being thought worthless or incapable, causes you to struggle with deceit, hiding parts of yourself you don't want others to see and forcing you to always portray a successful exterior. In doing so, you become unaware of who you are in your own heart, which impacts not only you, but also those in a relationship with you.

When trying to satisfy your longing for success and admiration apart from Christ, you can become excessively driven and image-conscious. Self-promotion, being competitive, and constantly comparing yourself to others, along with believing you are only as good as your last accomplishment, can lead you to burnout.

However, when your heart is aligned with the gospel, you believe that you are loved and valued for who you really are and not for only your successes and accomplishments. Your contagious confidence, enthusiasm, and focus inspires those around you. You become a humble, inner-directed team player who champions the people around you. Using your adaptability, productiveness, and drive for excellence, you achieve incredible things for the greater good.

Primary Perspective

- You believe love comes only from being or appearing successful; therefore, you avoid failure at all costs and shape-shift into appearing successful.
- You tend to embellish the truth, hoping others will see you only as successful, admirable, valuable, efficient, and accomplished. The slightest appearance of failure is terrifying.
- When you are struggling in life, you might double your efforts to appear successful by dressing well, owning more expensive items, and boasting of anything that would make you look better.

TYPE 3

Core Motivations

Core Fear: Being exposed as or thought incompetent, inefficient, or worthless; failing to be or appear successful.

Core Desire: Having high status and respect, being admired, successful, and valuable.

Core Weakness: *Deceit*—Deceiving yourself into believing you are only the image you present to others; embellishing the truth by putting on a polished persona for everyone (including yourself) to see and admire.

Core Longing: "You are loved and valued for simply being you."

Childhood Patterns

Childhood Message: "It's not okay for you to have your own feelings and identity."

Message Your Heart Longs to Hear (Core Longing): "You are loved and valued for simply being you. You don't have to earn my love."

Type 3 as a Child

You grew up believing others would only love you if you were successful, valuable, and admirable. To you, second place was losing, which was unacceptable. Because you always had to be the best, you put aside your own feelings and true identity and shape-shifted into any image or persona your parents, teachers, coaches, and others accepted and admired. To determine your worth, you constantly measured the responses of others to assess if you had earned their love or admiration. This pursuit was and still is exhausting.

Wings

Type 3 Wing 2 (3w2)
"The Star"

- **In General:** Charming, likable, adaptable, engaging, confident, and people-oriented with incredible interpersonal skills; enjoys the spotlight and attention. Strives to be desirable and admirable; performs to earn the admiration of others.
- **When Struggling:** Extremely competitive, plagued by comparison, and insecure about how others (particularly family) reflect on you.
- **Both Types Blend Easily with Each Other:** Both types have amazing interpersonal skills that easily lure the attention, praise, and admiration of others.
- **Inspiring Quality:** Immediately able to see exactly how to make others feel special, seen, and supported.

Type 3 Wing 4 (3w4)
"The Professional"

- **In General:** Private, quieter, and focused on achieving recognition through work and personal status; more emotionally vulnerable and sensitive.
- **When Struggling:** More afraid of failing; stronger need for others to recognize your accomplishments, causing you to dazzle people by embellishing the truth and promoting your achievements.
- **Both Types Are in Conflict with Each Other:** The Type 3 charms others with false personas while the Type 4 demands authenticity.
- **Inspiring Quality:** Mastering your craft or skill with introspection and creativity.

Stress and Growth Paths

Stress | Type 3 moves toward Average to Unhealthy Type 9

- You lose motivation and ambition, suddenly disengaging, becoming indifferent, and disassociating by numbing out.
- You stop self-promoting, lowering your profile by merging and blending with conventional norms.

Growth | Type 3 moves toward Healthy side of Type 6

- You focus less on self and more on others' well-being, becoming more loyal, cooperative, and committed.
- You become aware of your feelings, revealing who you are behind your "achieving" mask.

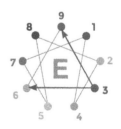

Levels of Alignment with the Gospel

Aligned (Living as His Beloved)
- Using your incredible talents and skills to solve problems in an efficient and productive way that benefits others as much as yourself.
- Helping others become the best versions of themselves instead of needing to win people over.
- Resting in your true identity in Christ and his accomplishments.
- Taking off your achieving mask so others can see your authentic self.
- Balancing work and family life well.
- Feeling, naming, and expressing your emotions openly with others.

Misaligned (Living in Our Own Strength)
- Believing you must earn love and admiration by becoming the most successful, admired, and respected individual.
- Focusing on being the very best in every category of life.
- Shape-shifting instantly into the right image to get admiration and praise from others.
- Experiencing and expressing a surplus of confidence.
- Prioritizing success so highly that you hide your emotions from yourself and others.
- Valuing work or accomplishments in a way that strains your family ties and friendships.

Out of Alignment (Living as an Orphan)
- Believing your worth hinges on your accomplishments, successes, and people's opinions of you.
- Constantly boasting, fabricating, and embellishing stories about yourself and your accomplishments to gain admiration from others.
- Refusing to admit when you are wrong or to reveal anything that diminishes your image; constantly presenting a favorable or admirable image, which is exhausting.
- Looking out for yourself alone; becoming extremely competitive, cruel, and vindictive.
- Harming everyone with your deceptiveness.

Instead of living in bondage to image, surrender to the Holy Spirit and depend on him completely. He will align you with the gospel, where you'll find true freedom and rest.

Communication Style
Motivator | Self-Promoting | Self-Assured | Efficient

Your Communication Tendencies

When you are doing well, you are clear, straightforward, confident, encouraging, and efficient; you focus on finding solutions and motivating others.

When you are NOT doing well, you can be irritated, self-promoting, impatient with emotional and lengthy conversations, brief when frustrated, and not fully willing to disclose what's really going on inside you.

Growth Areas for a Type 3's Communication Style
- Recognize that others may not be as driven, quick, and efficient as you.
- Demonstrate understanding, patience, and acceptance through encouragement and motivating words.
- Speak gently and with empathy; provide space for others to have their emotions when you give them feedback.
- Focus on others by asking them about their lives; show them you hear them and care by reflecting back to them what you heard.

Conflict Style

Common Conflict Activators
- Being blamed for someone else's bad performance or work
- Not looking good; being embarrassed
- Not being validated, affirmed, recognized, or praised for accomplishments
- Being put in a situation where failure is a high probability

Growth Areas for a Type 3's Conflict Style
- Be patient when others are not as quick or efficient as you.
- Don't force others to achieve or conform to a particular image to bolster your image.
- Demonstrate that people's emotions matter to you by intently listening to them.
- Create real work/life balance so your loved ones know they are valuable and important to you.
- Focus more on others' well-being.
- Be honest, transparent, and genuine in all matters.

Gospel Transformation

Christ Satisfies Your Core Longing

You long to hear, "You are loved for simply being you. You don't have to earn my love," yet no matter how much people try to satisfy this longing, they cannot. But Christ did and did so specifically for you as a Type 3 in these ways:

TYPE 3

1. **You are valued:** God demonstrated that he values you by sending his son to accomplish what you could not—your salvation. Your failures do not equal your value. Your Father values and cherishes you because of Christ's accomplishments on your behalf. Therefore, you do not need to earn your value through your accomplishments anymore.

2. **You are loved:** God invites you to be honest, transparent, and genuine, revealing your true self rather than an image or persona. He calls you to rest in your true identity in Christ and trust in his love for you without fearing what people think. Focus only on what he thinks of you . . . he simply loves you!

Growth Path for the Type 3
- Enjoy accomplishing goals for God's glory and others' benefit; you no longer need to strive to accomplish a particular status because you already have Christ's perfect status. Balance your work and life; because your status is secure in Christ, you no longer need to be the best or most accomplished at work or put your work before your family.
- Find at least one friend you can trust with complete honesty and see that you are loved even when you are not always presenting the most favorable image.
- Explore and experience what being Christ's valued and loved child is really about. Experiment and learn how to have real rest and solitude without needing to accomplish anything by finding something that is not about achieving but simply resting in the grace and love of Christ. You no longer need to "do," you now get to "be."

Understanding Them

Helpful Insight to Understand a Type 3

Type 3s are incredible at projecting an admirable and successful image and making the appearance of having it all together look effortless. But underneath the image, they have deep anxieties about their own personal worth and value. They worry that if they do not maintain a certain status, position, or image, others will devalue, reject, or toss them to the side as worthless.

This fear fuels their constant striving for improving themselves, accomplishing tasks, setting goals, and achieving success. They must always display a favorable appearance and perform at maximum efficiency. Others never suspect the degree of anxiety, insecurity, and loneliness that torments Threes, who constantly portray a likable, accomplished, efficient, and successful image.

Recognize Behavior Tendencies When a Type 3 is Activated

An activated Type 3 can:
- Disconnect their head from their heart and focus primarily on achieving rather than relating.
- Control body language to hide their emotions.
- Speak sharply in short sentences from a desire to solve issues quickly and efficiently.
- Begin to ask questions, think fast, and make decisions quickly.

Ways to Improve Communication with a Type 3 Spouse

- Do not interrupt a Three to talk about an issue when they are focused or working.
- Give them specific and clear examples of what you want them to accomplish and the time frame when you desire it completed; ambivalence in your desires slows them down and frustrates them.
- Encourage and affirm them often; be their number one supporter by setting them up to succeed.
- Be positive, develop a clear outline, and plan what the positive outcome needs to be for any difficult discussion.

How to Relate to a Type 3 in Conflict

- Come with a problem-solving approach.
- Keep your emotions balanced; do not exaggerate your negative or pessimistic emotions.

TYPE 3

- Reiterate that they are loved for who they are and not what they do or accomplish. But also affirm them on the good they did accomplish so they are not left wondering.
- Show love and acceptance for their authentic self rather than dwelling on their image and successes.
- Focus on the positive ways the Three can address your concerns instead of focusing on negative qualities or failures.
- Remind the Three specifically why and how they are valuable.

Type 3s Are at Their Best When They:
- Are self-accepting, authentic, modest, charitable, and able to experience their emotions.
- Take off their achieving masks to be known authentically, knowing their self-worth and value comes from Christ's perfect achievements on their behalf.
- Find satisfaction in the image they now have in Christ and no longer need to perform to earn love and admiration.
- Create a good work and family balance.
- Motivate others to become their best selves; stop comparing themselves with others' accomplishments.

Affirm Your Type 3 Spouse When They:
- Reveal their true feelings and who they are behind their "achieving masks."
- Commit to others' well-being, not just their successful image.
- Rely on Christ's accomplishments for them without embellishing their achievements or image.

How to Love Your Type 3 Better
- Say you love them for simply being themselves and not for what they do or accomplish (but still continue to affirm their accomplishments).
- Don't distract or interrupt them while they are focused or working.
- Keep conversations constructive and feedback positive rather than overly critical or emotional.
- Provide tidy and peaceful surroundings where they can thrive.
- Remind them that their value and worth is not in what they accomplish but in what Christ accomplished for them.
- Give your Three time and grace as they discover who their authentic self really is inside.
- Encourage and affirm them when you see them living out of their genuine self.

TYPE 4

Type 4: The Romantic Individualist

Authentic | Creative | Expressive | Deep | Temperamental

Understanding Me

Summary of Type 4: The Romantic Individualist is authentic, creative, expressive, deep, temperamental.

You are a creative force with a knack for discovering beauty, originality, and value in places that others miss. Your rich interior life of thoughts and feelings creates a hunger in you for emotional intensity and authenticity. Although you see profound despair and suffering in the world, you also see joy and you bravely press into hard depths to discover meaning in all of life. You embrace a wide range of emotions and experiences, and with your knack for self-expression, you bring a unique aesthetic, depth, and creativity to any event or situation.

Just as you are eager to explore the depths of our complicated world in a search for meaning and genuine connections, you also look inside yourself to find your own unique significance and value. However, when looking into your heart, a constant feeling burdens you that you are missing something important and that you're flawed in ways no one else is. Craving ideal circumstances or love, you often cannot stop pondering what is missing in your life and exploring this sense of disconnectedness. Struggling with feelings of envy, you compare yourself to others, longing for what you don't have and believing others have what you long to possess.

When you attempt to find your unique significance and individuality apart from Christ, you can become self-absorbed and temperamental, perpetually seeing your weakness and never your glory. Painfully self-conscious, you spend a great deal of energy ruminating in your mind on how different you are from others and navigating feelings of self-hatred, shame, emptiness, and despair. You may be anxious around others, always wondering what they think about you.

Beyond your internal strife, you can get into relational conflicts by being withholding, dramatic, and temperamental; at times you may appear self-absorbed and disinterested in others.

However, when you take the longings of your heart to Christ and step out from under the waterfall of your emotions, you bring forth your talents in ways that are truly extraordinary. You have a deep intuition for how others feel and can step into turbulent feelings with ease and compassion; they don't overwhelm you. In fact, connecting with others and their intense emotions, and being there for them in their pain, brings you great joy. With your creativity, imagination, and authentic self-expression, you are an amazing gift to the world.

Primary Perspective

- You feel and believe you are tragically flawed and that others possess qualities you lack.
- This belief causes shameful feelings of inferiority, which lead to envy.
- Constantly comparing what others have and what you sense you are lacking further isolates you and makes you feel like you are misunderstood and do not belong.
- This puts you on a never-ending journey to find what you are missing inside in hopes that others will understand and love you for being your unique and special self.

Core Motivations

Core Fear: Being inadequate, emotionally cut off, plain, mundane, defective, flawed, or insignificant.
Core Desire: Being unique, special, and finding your authentic self.

Core Weakness: *Envy*—Feeling that you're tragically flawed, something foundational is missing inside you, and others possess qualities you lack.
Core Longing: "You are seen and loved for exactly who you are— special and unique."

Childhood Patterns

Childhood Message: "It's not okay to be too much or not enough."

Message Your Heart Longs to Hear (Core Longing):
"You are seen and loved for exactly who you are—special and unique."

The Type 4 as a Child

Growing up, you felt disconnected from both your parents to some degree; they misunderstood you. Feeling misunderstood led you to assume there was something fundamentally missing or tragically flawed within you. So, you believed you needed to find something different and unique about you to stand out so others would see you and have a reason to love you.

Discovering your authentic and unique self then became your primary focus in life. Longings, feelings, and passions ran deep within you. You used your emotions as the primary source to build your unique identity.

Wings

Type 4 Wing 3 (4w3)
"The Bohemian"

- **In General:** Refined taste, emotionally vivid and buoyant, extroverted, upbeat, goal-oriented, and interpersonal.
- **When Struggling:** More consumed with what others think of you, envying what others have that you feel you lack; more emotional fluctuations.
- **Both Types Are in Conflict with Each Other:** Type 4 desires authenticity and true self-expression, but the Type 3 needs validation of accomplishments and shape-shifts into the most admirable image.
- **Inspiring Quality:** Establishing your own unique mark on the world with your creativity, originality, and ambition.

Type 4 Wing 5 (4w5)
"The Aristocrat"

- **In General:** Intellectually deep, creative, original, introverted, isolated, less ambitious, and less concerned with what others think.
- **When Struggling:** More withdrawn, fiercely independent, and consumed by your emotional and intellectual worlds; must sort out your emotions by using more of your intellect before you can move forward.
- **Both Types Blend Easily with Each Other:** Both are withdrawn types. Type 4s withdraw to protect your emotions, and Type 5s to protect your inner resources.
- **Inspiring Quality:** Remarkably creative, unusual, mysterious, and eccentric, you combine intellectual insights with emotional intuition to produce stunning original works.

Stress and Growth Paths

Stress | Type 4 moves toward Average to Unhealthy Type 2
- You suddenly cling to others, becoming overly-involved and manipulating others into loving you.
- You believe your emptiness and loneliness will go away if you gain the attention of others.

Growth | Type 4 moves toward Healthy side of Type 1
- Your turbulent emotions become more balanced, objective, and principled.
- You become more disciplined, focused, and productive when you see the importance of doing what is right.

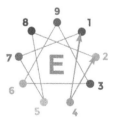

Levels of Alignment with the Gospel

Aligned (Living as His Beloved)

- Enjoying creativity, inspiring others, and experiencing your emotions with balance.
- Believing God unconditionally loves you, perfectly understands you, and created you exactly the way he desired—special and unique.
- Letting go of envy, not comparing yourself to others, and realizing you are not lacking anything; you have all of Christ's spiritual blessings, forgiveness, and righteousness.
- Acknowledging that everything your heart feels is missing, you now have in Christ all of the time. You no longer have to search for what is missing.
- Feeling secure in his love and knowing he will never abandon you.

Misaligned (Living in Our Own Strength)

- Feeling the need to exaggerate your uniqueness in order to get attention and affection from others because you have begun to forget Christ's great love for you.
- Believing you are missing something foundational inside that others have, which causes you to envy others for having what you feel you are missing.
- Searching constantly for your unique self in your internal world of emotions and imagination.
- Feeling lonely and misunderstood by others.

Out of Alignment (Living as an Orphan)

- Believing you are unlovable and not valued for your authentic self.
- Striving harder to be unique and set apart for others to see you and value you.
- Feeling misunderstood, defective, flawed, and utterly alone when others do not understand your unique style.
- Plunging into sadness, despair, and self-absorption; being temperamental and moody; feeling no one will ever understand you and love you for your unique self.

Instead of living in bondage to uniqueness, surrender to the Holy Spirit and depend on him completely, and he will align you with the gospel, where you'll find true freedom and rest.

TYPE 4

TYPE 4

Communication Style
Deep | Expressive | Meaningful | Authentic

Your Communication Tendencies

When you are doing well, you are authentic, deep, empathetic, and a great listener when others are sad or suffering; you express your emotions with inner balance.

When you are NOT doing well, you can be moody, emotionally intense, and explosive; or cold, detached, and condescending; you will steer the conversation to focus on you.

Growth Areas for a Type 4's Communication Style
- Realize that not understanding you doesn't mean others don't care or are insensitive.
- Mirror other people's moods and conversations back to them instead of just focusing on yours.
- Be patient when others are slower to express their emotions than you.
- Allow others to experience their emotions in the way that is comfortable to them.

Conflict Style

Common Conflict Activators
- Being asked to do something that is contrary to who you are or your values
- Feeling anything that evokes your struggle with envy
- Not being seen as unique, special, or different
- Not being valued for your unique contributions or viewpoints

Growth Areas for a Type 4's Conflict Style
- Learn how to navigate your emotions and bring them into balance so you can clearly express yourself in more understandable ways. You don't need to feel less emotions in order to work through conflicts with others.
- Track and understand what activates you into conflict inside.
- Don't allow your emotions to pull you into a false reality; remain emotionally balanced so you can deal with feelings in a more grounded way.

Gospel Transformation

Christ Satisfies Your Core Longing

You long to hear, "You are seen and loved for exactly who you are—special and unique," yet no matter how much people try to satisfy this longing, they cannot. But Christ did and did so specifically for you as a Type 4 in these ways:

1. **You are seen:** Not only does Christ see all your unique abilities that reflect him, he also sees your depravity. He sees your sorrows and needs. He came specifically to rescue you because he saw you had a need that was too great for you to bear. Only he could rescue you from this fallen world and from yourself. He delights in seeing you and coming to your rescue with his great love.

2. **You are understood:** You feel misunderstood and different, but the good news is that God completely understands, loves, and cherishes you for exactly who you are. God created you uniquely, and he delights in his own creativity. Knowing this, you can fully rest in the truth that you are seen and loved for exactly who you are!

Growth Path for the Type 4

- Rest your emotions and identity in being his beloved and cherished child whom he already finds delight in knowing deeply and intimately.
- Bless others with the radiance, creativity, and individuality given to you.
- Embrace this truth: You BELONG! You are not too much or not enough. Christ secured your place with him. He sees you, values you, and loves you deeply.
- Accept that you are not your emotions; you are God's beloved child. Your emotions fluctuate, but your identity in Christ remains exactly the same.
- Realize that you can only see a small portion of the glorious, mysterious tapestry that God is creating. At best, you can only see the underside, but one day you will see its fullness and beauty. You will see how every thread played an important and vital part in his masterpiece. You will see your unique and glorious role. For now, rest and be delighted in the fact that he wants you to participate in this work with him. God has designed your life to bring him glory and to bless you.

TYPE 4

Understanding Them

Helpful Insight to Understand a Type 4

Deep down, Fours have a hidden, idealized self—a self they passionately desire to become. This idealized self is incredibly creative, socially adept, and universally desired. They compare themselves to this idealized self and see how they are defective and flawed. They believe no one will truly love them the way they are, so they strive more and more to become this idealized self in order to be loved.

Because they are constantly comparing themselves to this false self, their imagination causes these false realities to become larger than life with no hope for resolution. Then they can despair and become hopeless in their feelings and assumptions. Growth for a Four involves letting go of this idealized self and learning to value and appreciate who they actually are—uniquely created, pursued, saved, seen, and loved deeply by their Savior.

Recognize Behavior Tendencies When a Type 4 is Activated

An activated Type 4 can:
- Become either withdrawn and quiet or likely to voice their feelings and opinions bluntly.
- Feel they need to work through a multitude of feelings within and understand them before they can move forward.
- Try intensely to get others to understand their perspective and feelings.
- Hold onto their feelings and moods for a long time.

Ways to Improve Communication with a Type 4 Spouse
- Express your emotions more openly to develop a solid and meaningful emotional relationship.
- Be authentic and real or communication with a Four will stall and cease to exist.
- Encourage a Four to express their emotions with clarity and balance instead of telling them not to have emotions or limiting their experience or expression of feeling.
- Express what you admire and appreciate about a Four; do not try to change them.
- Mirror back to them their own beautiful reflection so they know you see them.
- Remind them that Christ perfectly made them, and nothing is missing in them.

TYPE 4

How to Relate to a Type 4 in Conflict
- Be patient and accepting, because Type 4s can take a long time to express the depths of their emotions fully.
- Reassure them and listen until they are completely finished expressing themselves so they feel valued and validated.
- Paraphrase what they were trying to communicate when they are done sharing to see if you understood them. If you did not understand them correctly, ask for clarification. Repeat until you understand them fully.
- Do not suggest to them or tell them they are being overly sensitive or dramatic, which will only hurt and isolate them, making them withdraw.

Type 4s Are at Their Best When They:
- Are self-aware, introspective, creative, gentle, compassionate, empathetic, and intuitive with both themselves and others.
- Balance emotion when expressing themselves, transforming all their experiences into something beautiful and valuable.
- Marvel at the depth of Christ's love for them and allow it to inspire them to be more like him.
- Rest in the truth that Christ will never leave them, feeling understood and loved.
- See their significance through the eyes of their Creator, which renews their souls.

Affirm Your Type 4 Spouse When They:
- Display emotional balance.
- Believe that nothing inside them is missing, accepting that they're complete and whole in Christ.
- Acknowledge that God completely understands them and cherishes them.
- Trust that Christ fully sees them, knows them, and loves them for exactly who they are.

How to Love Your Type 4 Better
- Be tender, empathetic, and understanding without trying to change them into what you want them to be.
- Tell them what you truly see and appreciate about them (but do not flatter).
- Reinforce that there is nothing missing in them and they were created with the beautiful qualities God intended for them to have.
- See their valuable gift of intuition, vision, and creativity.
- Allow them space to feel their emotions and even ask them about them. Don't tell them to get out of a melancholy mood, say they are being too sensitive, or accuse them of overreacting.
- Remind them that they are loved and cherished deeply for exactly who they are.

TYPE 4

Type 5: The Investigative Thinker

Perceptive | Insightful | Intelligent | Detached | Isolated

Understanding Me

Summary of Type 5: The Investigative Thinker is perceptive, insightful, intelligent, detached, isolated.

You are a perceptive, innovative observer who walks through life with curiosity, craving to learn new things. Your inquisitive mind is objective and practical, making wise decisions based on reason and knowledge.

Despite your insatiable thirst for thinking and knowing, you experience the world as an intrusive and overwhelming place. Feeling that life demands too much of you, you focus your attention on conserving your energy and resources, fearing being empty and experiencing a sense of catastrophic depletion. This intense desire to hoard and control your resources and environment challenges you and your relationships, as you can become extremely private and emotionally distant.

When you attempt to navigate life apart from Christ, your fear of being incompetent and unknowledgeable, coupled with your desire for self-sufficiency and reluctance to rely on others, can cause you to withdraw, isolate, and become emotionally distant. You often feel you must know everything before sharing your insights, and your fear of feeling incompetent overwhelms you and causes you to retreat.

This desire for knowledge, independence, and a life free from obligations can strain your relationships, which require connection, feelings, and vulnerability to be healthy. You see your spouse and their needs, but you feel ill-equipped to meet them, often perceiving them as demands. So, you distance yourself from relationships in hopes that eventually you'll feel competent enough to engage. You wonder if you'll ever be able to have enough knowledge or resources to enter the mysterious and complex world of another person.

Fortunately, when your heart is aligned with the gospel, you discover that your needs are not a problem because Christ has fulfilled them. Then you can begin to be more generous with giving of yourself and your resources to others, moving from a fear of scarcity to a belief in abundance. You begin living not just from your head but from your heart, and the whole of who you are. That, coupled with your great vision and perspective, reflects true wisdom for the world.

Primary Perspective

- You think the more knowledge you can obtain, the more security and independence you will experience.
- You perceive the world and other people as intrusive and overwhelming, draining your already limited energy resources. Without time alone, you fear you will experience catastrophic depletion.
- To preserve your energy resources, you withdraw from people and detach from your emotions until you can recharge alone.
- You have a special, private location where you can truly be alone to recharge and process your thoughts and feelings.
- Establishing and maintaining boundaries is important to you and your well-being.

Core Motivations

Core Fear: Being annihilated, invaded, or not existing; being thought incapable or ignorant; having obligations placed upon you or your energy depleted.

Core Desire: Being knowledgeable, capable, and competent.

Core Weakness: Avarice—Feeling you lack inner resources and that too much interaction with others will lead to catastrophic depletion; withholding yourself from contact with the world; holding onto your resources and minimizing your needs.

Core Longing: "Your needs are not a problem."

TYPE 5

Childhood Patterns

Childhood Message: "It's not okay to be comfortable in the world."

Message Your Heart Longs to Hear (Core Longing): "Your needs are not a problem."

Type 5 as a Child

Growing up, you preferred observing the world to actively participating in it, and you enjoyed retreating into the world of your mind. You found comfort and safety like a fortress in your mind. It felt safer to keep your thoughts and feelings to yourself, so you remained more private and isolated than other kids. You tended to keep people and the world, which were overwhelming and energy-depleting, at a safe distance. The distance helped you not to feel overwhelmed and drained by outside forces.

Wings

Type 5 Wing 4 (5w4)
"The Iconoclast"

- **In General:** Withdrawn, isolated, eccentric; more emotional, creative, and imaginative.
- **When Struggling:** Detach from others by using their intellectual insights and observations to create distance but are more sensitive than people realize.
- **Both Types Blend Easily with Each Other:** Both withdrawn types; moves inward toward their intellect and emotions. Both isolate—the Type 5 for thinking they are incompetent and Type 4 for feeling something is fundamentally missing in them.
- **Inspiring Quality:** Amazing ability to pull things apart and then conceptualize new ways to look at it from a creative viewpoint.

Type 5 Wing 6 (5w6)
"The Problem Solver"

- **In General:** Intellectual, cerebral, observant, analyzing, and problem-solving.
- **When Struggling:** Mainly live in their minds and not their emotions; intimate or personal relationships can be difficult and challenging.
- **Both Types Are in Conflict with Each Other:** Relationships are not top priority or easy to navigate with the Type 5 finding security through detaching and withdrawing from others and the Type 6 desiring to work collaboratively with others to find their security.
- **Inspiring Quality:** Thrives on dissecting problems, analyzing them, and finding a solution through their research and intellectual power.

Stress and Growth Paths

Stress | Type 5 moves toward Average to Unhealthy Type 7

- You become scattered and excitable, taking on new projects quickly and without thought.
- You become unfocused and distracted with too many new possibilities in front of you.

Growth | Type 5 moves toward Healthy side of Type 8

- You trust your instincts and become more assertive, self-confident, decisive, and prone to act.
- You become physically active, which connects your thinking to your emotions and gut.

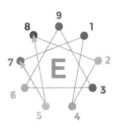

Levels of Alignment with the Gospel

Aligned (Living as His Beloved)
- Generating tremendous insights and understanding.
- Observing new things that most people cannot see or do not notice.
- Creating great innovations, new bodies of knowledge, and radical inventions that will benefit the world.
- Feeling deeply connected with yourself and others; using your knowledge and insight to help others.
- Knowing Christ will replenish your depleted reserves and take care of your needs.

Misaligned (Living in Our Own Strength)
- Forgetting Christ will supply all your needs.
- Fearing that if you share your needs with others, they will reject you, overwhelm you, and intrude on your space.
- Putting up strong boundaries to protect yourself from people becoming too invasive.
- Withdrawing to remain private, guarded, and autonomous.
- Detaching yourself from your emotions and hoarding your internal resources to avoid being depleted.

Out of Alignment (Living as an Orphan)
- Focusing primarily on withdrawing, isolating, and hoarding your resources.
- Allowing your mind to veer off and becoming frightened by your own deep, haunting, and conspiratorial thinking.
- Fearing others are planning to harm you.
- Becoming subject to distorted thoughts.
- Isolating yourself and detaching from reality.

TYPE 5

Instead of living in bondage to isolation, surrender to the Holy Spirit and depend on him completely, and he will align you with the gospel, where you'll find true freedom and rest.

Communication Style
Intellectual | Data | Brief | Lecture

Your Communication Tendencies

When you are doing well, you are respectful, non-intrusive, curious, and observant; you engage in stimulating conversations with others.

When you are NOT doing well, you can be overly brief, cold, and intellectually arrogant. You might withdraw or detach when you feel relational obligations placed on you.

Growth Areas for a Type 5's Communication Style
- Learn to ask others for help where you need it. Yes, we are called to let others help us carry our burdens (Galatians 6:2–5).
- Purposefully engage with others and the world, trusting that God will provide all you need (your energy reserves) instead of defaulting to withdrawing from others.
- Raise your awareness of what others need and feel.
- Bring your emotions outward so others can experience relational warmth.

Conflict Style

Common Conflict Activators
- Being given overwhelming tasks
- Being a victim of broken confidentiality or dishonesty
- Feeling surprise, intrusion, and obligation
- Lacking privacy to recharge and process your thoughts and feelings

Growth Areas for a Type 5's Conflict Style
- Express your feelings more often during conflict, not just your thoughts.
- Communicate your need to process your thoughts and feelings alone in a way that is not threatening so you can come back to the conversation with a fuller perspective and more energy.
- Learn to read nonverbal cues, as people communicate a great deal during a conflict just by their body language.

Gospel Transformation

Christ Satisfies Your Core Longing

You long to hear, "Your needs are not a problem," yet no matter how much people try to satisfy this longing, they cannot. But Christ did and did so specifically for you as a Type 5 in these ways:

1. **Your needs are seen and taken care of:** You do not need to worry that your resources will run out. Christ knows exactly what you need and provides for you out of his immense love for you.

2. **Christ replenishes your empty internal reservoir:** Christ knows your relational battery gets drained quickly, and you need solitude to recharge and to process your thoughts and feelings. Go to him in solitude, and he will recharge and replenish you with more satisfying energy! He will give you what you need. To pour out blessings on you is not a burden for him but a delight. Receive and be filled.

Growth Path for the Type 5

- Practice giving your time and resources to others as a step of faith that God will replenish them in the exact way you need.
- Let go of the belief that you must be completely self-sufficient. Instead, use God's community to support and care for you.
- Take a step of faith and seek relationships that will be mutually beneficial.
- Allow for mystery in life, trusting God will reveal truths and knowledge when he sees fit.
- Practice believing you have abundance instead of scarcity.
- Know that all you need is given to you, with more to come.
- Trust that God has enough resources, energy, relationships, and love to go around. God, who is not short on resources, has all you need and blesses each of his children perfectly.
- Practice being more open and sharing with others you trust.

TYPE 5

Understanding Them

Helpful Insight to Understand a Type 5

Fives feel they lack inner resources and that too much interaction with others will lead to catastrophic depletion of their energy reserves. Therefore, Fives isolate themselves from others, hold onto their resources, and minimize their needs. Think of their internal resources like a cell phone battery that only has 20% battery life max every day. They have to ration their usage so it lasts until they can recharge it. To others, their strong boundaries and need for privacy to recharge might come across as being impersonal, but it is vital for processing and regaining their energy levels to be able to interact with others again.

Recognize Behavior Tendencies When a Type 5 is Activated

An activated Type 5 can:

- Become withdrawn and quiet or angry and enraged if others are cornering them and not respecting their boundaries.
- Detach and isolate themselves from others by not showing emotions.
- Detach emotions and observe their surroundings but later process their emotions privately.
- Come across as intellectually arrogant.

Ways to Improve Communication with a Type 5 Spouse

- Keep the conversation focused on facts and specific details.
- Understand that Fives can't always drum up their thoughts and emotions on the spot and may need more time alone to process them fully before expressing them to you.
- Inform the Five how long the conversation will take. This helps them manage their internal resources.
- Ask them what percentage of energy they have left so you can demonstrate that you understand their needs.
- Tell them what you want to discuss in advance to give them time to start processing.
- Allow time and space for the Five to digest and process the information and their feelings.

How to Relate to a Type 5 in Conflict
- Keep your conversations with a Five private and confidential. They are extremely private people who hold the information others give them with absolute confidentiality and expect you will do the same.
- Respect the limited internal resources Fives have on any given day. Surprises and intrusions will quickly drain them.
- Make them aware of anything that might drain them ahead of time.
- Be aware of what depletes your Five and remove it. Provide a safe space for them to process their thoughts.

Type 5s Are at Their Best When They:
- See what could be and bring together a wide range of knowledge to pioneer new ways of doing things that bless others.
- Remain extremely observant, perceptive, alert, and curious.
- Bring powerful insights to any topic at hand.
- Use their amazing ability to stay focused in order to become engrossed in learning.
- Interact with people more, knowing Christ will fill up their internal reservoir when there is a need.

Affirm Your Type 5 Spouse When They:
- Allow themselves to need others and express their needs to others.
- Connect to others and express their feelings.
- Trust God to replenish them so they can engage with people more.
- Assert themselves with confidence.

How to Love Your Type 5 Better
- Become more independent and not clingy.
- Keep conversations straightforward and to the point. Being brief is better and less exhausting to them.
- Give them their own space, time, and privacy so they can recharge without interruption. They simply have a need to recharge privately (just like our phones need to be plugged into an outlet) to be able to interact more in relationships.
- Provide for them in an unobtrusive way when you see they have a need. Asking for help is really difficult for Fives.
- Do not share with others what they have privately shared with you. Trust and confidentiality are extremely important to them.

Type 6: The Loyal Guardian

Committed | Responsible | Faithful | Suspicious | Anxious

Understanding Me

Summary of Type 6: The Loyal Guardian is committed, responsible, faithful, suspicious, anxious.

You are one of the steadiest and most reliable, hardworking, and dutiful people out there. Your dependability, sense of humor, and ability to foresee problems cause you to be an incredible team player. Truly concerned about the common good, you can hold groups together.

However, below the surface, constant fear and uncertainty often plague you so that you experience the world as a dangerous place where you must be hyper-vigilant, scanning for things that could threaten your safety, security, and relationships. Whether to avoid danger or challenge it head on, you can be prone to see and assume the worst. You manage your anxiety by preemptively running through worst-case scenarios to prepare for whatever bad might possibly happen. Inside your mind is a constant refrain of, "But what about this . . ., what about that...?"

When you forget the truth of the gospel, you can suffer from self-doubt, worry, and catastrophic thinking, which leaves you feeling anxious and costs you your ability to relax and trust yourself and others. Your mind can become muddled, skeptical, and hesitant to make decisions. You will focus on planning for crises to give you a sense of control, safety, and security in your attempt to live in a world that is trouble-free and predictable.

In relationships, you can struggle with projecting your fears, doubts, and insecurities onto others as a means to protect yourself. The challenge is that these misplaced fears, suspicions, and doubts often erode your trust in other people, God, and yourself.

However, when your heart is aligned with the gospel and you learn to take your fears and anxiety to Christ, you experience a transformation that brings forth great courage in your life. As you realize you are secure in him, you begin to trust yourself more, and you experience a peace that surpasses the fears you see in the world around you. Beyond that, the world is blessed by your dedication, wit, ability to solve problems and genuine loyalty.

TYPE 6

Primary Perspective

- You believe the world is a dangerous place and that most people have hidden agendas.
- You constantly scan the horizon to predict and plan for all possible outcomes (especially worst-case scenarios) and to prevent potential harm from occurring.
- You believe if you can rehearse in your mind what might happen and develop strategies to prevent negative circumstances (physical or relationship-oriented) from occurring, then you can keep yourself and others safe and secure.

Core Motivations

Core Fear: Feeling fear itself, being without support, security, or guidance; being blamed, targeted, alone, or physically abandoned.

Core Desire: Having security, guidance, and support.

Core Weakness: Anxiety—Scanning the horizon of life and trying to predict and prevent negative outcomes (especially worst-case scenarios); remaining in a constant state of apprehension and worry.

Core Longing: "You are safe and secure."

TYPE 6

Childhood Patterns

Childhood Message: "It's not okay to trust or depend on yourself."

Message Your Heart Longs to Hear (Core Longing): "You are safe and secure."

The Type 6 as a Child

Growing up, you desired guidance, support, and security, but you felt the world was a dangerous and unreliable place. In order to avoid potential harm, chaos, or insecurity, you learned to predict, strategize, and plan what could go wrong.

Your "inner committee" started at an early age, informing you of every possible outcome to ensure safety and security. Instead, your inner committee brought uncertainty and confusion by creating a great degree of self-doubt in decision-making. This caused you to seek clear and reliable guidance and advice from authority figures you trusted to help you feel safe and secure.

Wings

Type 6 Wing 5 (6w5)
"The Defender"

- **In General:** Organized, perceptive, cerebral, withdrawn, and knowledgeable; self-controlled, responsible, and serious about ethical and political beliefs (can be mistyped as a 1); outspoken and intense (can look like an 8).
- **When Struggling:** More suspicious and isolated while watching for potential adversaries.
- **Both Types Are in Conflict with Each Other:** Type 6 wants to band together with others for security and support, while Type 5 looks to detach from others to maintain internal resources.
- **Inspiring Quality:** A mindful voice for the underdogs who will go to great lengths to defend them.

Type 6 Wing 7 (6w7)
"The Buddy"

- **In General:** Engaging, supportive, witty, sociable, and likable; looking to team up with others for extra support and security.
- **When Struggling:** More anxious and hardworking yet procrastinates out of fear. More reactive when experiencing anxiety and internal pressure to make decisions quickly.
- **Both Types Blend Easily with Each Other:** Both are extroverted, highly sociable, enjoy having a good time with trusted and committed friends, and finding new connections to ensure security and fun times together.
- **Inspiring Quality:** A very thoughtful, warm, and engaging friend who constantly looks out for problems but wants to have loads of fun as well.

Stress and Growth Paths

Stress | Type 6 moves toward Average to Unhealthy Type 3
- You arrogantly think you alone see all possible scenarios while believing others do not see reality.
- You stay busy to avoid feeling anxious, and you're reluctant to try something if failure is a possibility.

Growth | Type 6 moves toward Healthy side of Type 9
- You take life a little less seriously, allowing your mind to slow down so you can relax more and enjoy the moment.
- You can empathize with others more and extend compassion to them.

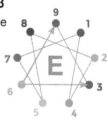

Levels of Alignment with the Gospel

Aligned (Living as His Beloved)

- Taking your anxieties and insecurities to God, knowing he is both able and faithful to care for you. This allows your mind to stop racing and calm down.
- Placing your trust in him instead of trying to predict and control life on your own.
- Understanding there is never certainty of safety and security on earth, but you can trust that God will always be there to love, protect, and provide for you.
- Remaining warm, loving, witty, engaging, trusting, and playful.
- Thinking of others and enjoying collaborating with a group or team.
- Following through on your commitments and troubleshooting problems.

Misaligned (Living in Our Own Strength)

- Believing you are alone and need to scan the horizon for dangers and people who might harm you.
- Taking control of situations because no one else is as cautious and vigilant as you are.
- Questioning everything and everyone constantly to predict the future.
- Looking for a trustworthy authority figure to trust but testing them to see if they deserve your loyalty (creating the very problems you are trying to prevent).

Out of Alignment (Living as an Orphan)

- Remaining on constant lookout for dangers at every turn.
- Becoming hyper-vigilant and suspicious of everyone, leading you toward paranoia.
- Failing to trust your own thinking and decision-making ability or any authority figure, which ultimately makes you feel more alone, anxious, and cynical, and produces extreme anxiety and fear.

TYPE 6

Instead of living in bondage to security, surrender to the Holy Spirit and depend on him completely, and he will align you with the gospel, where you'll find true freedom and rest.

Communication Style
Supportive | Inquisitive | Cautious | Reactive
Your Communication Tendencies

When you are doing well, you are warm, caring, compassionate, witty, funny, and a good listener, and you like to engage in a healthy, two-way conversation.

When you are NOT doing well, you can be overly reactive, anxious, skeptical, and suspicious; you question others, not trusting anyone, and doubt them and yourself.

Growth Areas for a Type 6's Communication Style
- Allow your inner world to become calmer and less reactive before having significant conversations.
- Recognize the burden of responsibility ultimately does not rest solely on your shoulders.
- Offer balanced perspectives (benefits and concerns) on any given conversation.
- Seek truth by asking clarifying questions instead of using projection and making assumptions.

Conflict Style

Common Conflict Activators
- Being targeted, blamed, or accused unfairly
- Being put under pressure
- Seeing others not being genuine, authentic, and honest
- Seeing others lacking commitment, loyalty, and follow-through
- Being lied to or abandoned, or the appearance of either
- Seeing others not taking your anxieties or concerns seriously

Growth Areas for a Type 6's Conflict Style
- Manage your real source of anxiety: the contradictory thoughts and possibilities the "internal committee" voices to you.
- Experience silence and solitude with God to enable more clarity in making decisions more confidently.
- Listen to your "inner committee" respectfully, acknowledge their worries and concerns, and then inform them you will make a mature decision after weighing all the information and trusting the Holy Spirit to bring you the clarity, wisdom, insight, peace, assurance, and guidance you need to move forward with a confident decision.

- Trust in the Holy Spirit's provision to help you be more sober-minded instead of emotionally reactive.

Gospel Transformation

Christ Satisfies Your Core Longing

You long to hear, "You are safe and secure," yet no matter how much people try to satisfy this longing, they cannot. But Christ did and did so specifically for you as a Type 6 in these ways:

1. **God is all-powerful, and you are safe in his care:** You feel you are all alone and need to protect yourself from uncertainty and danger. You cannot accomplish this because you are finite, but God can and will protect you with his wisdom and strength because he loves you.

2. **The Holy Spirit gives you clarity and certainty in a confusing and chaotic world:** Your "inner committee" gives too many contradictory messages, causing confusion and doubt. The Holy Spirit gives clarity, peace, and assurance. He will assure you that you are not alone, but rather guided and directed in every way.

TYPE 6

Growth Path for the Type 6

- Spend regular time in silence and solitude so you can become acquainted with your "inner committee." Listen to them without reacting. Welcome their comments with a neutral position. You are not agreeing with them, but simply listening.
- Ask the Holy Spirit to guide you in knowing which thoughts to accept or discard.
- Write down your anxieties and fears when they rise within you so they are outside of you, give them to the Lord, and trust that the Holy Spirit will give you the insight and wisdom you need.
- Be aware of your tendency to have issues with authority. Consider how you can rest in God as your authority and not make a person into something they are not.
- Learn to have peace of mind versus being over-reactive.
- Learn when you are projecting onto others, apologize, and ask clarifying questions instead of making assumptions.

Understanding Them

Helpful Insight to Understand a Type 6

The real source of anxiety for Sixes is the "internal committee" of voices that are constantly chiming in with contradictory thoughts and a multitude of different possibilities, analyses, worst-case scenarios, and questions. This "inner committee" constantly causes them to second-guess themselves, doubt what they know, and consult others. It is nearly impossible for them to think clearly and decide when their minds are revved up in this hyper-vigilant state. Taking a listening and understanding stance will help settle reactions. Don't shame them for their anxieties, but instead reassure them you understand and offer support.

Recognize Behavior Tendencies When a Type 6 is Activated

An activated Type 6 can:

- Either fearfully withdraw or become highly reactive.
- Engage in intense mental analysis with any given situation or conflict.
- Believe their projections are accurate and real, leading them to redirect their own thoughts, feelings, and motives onto others.

Ways to Improve Communication with a Type 6 Spouse

- Be clear, direct, and specific on what you are thinking, feeling, and wanting when giving feedback. This keeps them from over-speculating or "catastrophizing" in their mind what you might say.
- Explain when you need some time to process your thoughts and feelings and assure the Six you will discuss the issue instead of fleeing from hard conversations, causing the Six to think of all the worst reasons and possibilities and leading them to more fear and anxiety.
- Reassure the Six of your support, love, and faithfulness before, after, and even during a heavy conversation.
- Create a safe relational atmosphere by often giving the Six support, assurance, and loyalty.

How to Relate to a Type 6 in Conflict

- Ask if they want to discuss the issue now or if they need time to process their thoughts.
- Allow them to share their thoughts while you remain a calm and steady presence.
- Listen to them first, reassure them, then give your honest and nonreactive perspective.
- Show loyalty and love by being warm, understanding, and supportive.

- Be a reassuring presence so they don't feel targeted, blamed, or abandoned.
- Rebuild broken trust, because trust and security are a top need for a Six.
- To build trust, demonstrate consistent loyalty, commitment, and truthfulness.

Type 6s Are at Their Best When They:
- Are self-affirming and courageous, trusting themselves and others.
- Remain endearing, warm, friendly, playful, witty, likable, deeply engaging, dependable, and committed.
- Treat everyone (including themselves) as an equal.
- Fiercely commit to their homes, jobs, and communities and strive to build stability and security there.
- Advocate for those who are powerless.
- Take anxieties and insecurities first to God and trust in his sovereignty and timing rather than their projections, assumptions, and predictions.

Affirm Your Type 6 Spouse When They:
- Trust that God will give them the clarity, courage, and strength they need to handle life's challenges.
- Rely on their own discernment and make a confident decision.
- Believe they are not alone or abandoned but are God's beloved child.

How to Love Your Type 6 Better
- Be honest, clear, and direct when you communicate.
- Help them feel secure by being committed, hardworking, responsible, and trustworthy.
- Demonstrate you're a safe place where they can share concerns without being judged for their anxiety.
- Show empathy, support, and understanding of their struggles with anxiety due to their vigilant "inner committee."
- Listen patiently to their perspective instead of forcing them to be optimistic.
- Reassure them that you are loyal and committed above all else.
- Remind them that God is loyal, committed, faithful, and protective, and they can always find refuge in him.

TYPE 6

Type 7: The Entertaining Optimist

Playful | Excitable | Versatile | Scattered | Escapist

Understanding Me

Summary of Type 7: The Entertaining Optimist is playful, excitable, versatile, scattered, escapist.

You are a joyful, enthusiastic, and social person who radiates optimism wherever you go. As a lover of variety, you live life "big." You're eager to enjoy all of the vast experiences this world has to offer, seeing innovation and endless possibilities everywhere.

While you bring happiness and a positive outlook wherever you go, internally you are always longing for "more" and fearful of missing out. To you, life is like cotton candy, tasting super sweet but disappearing quickly, leaving you constantly unsatisfied and wanting another bite, and then another bite. Additionally, life can be painful and hard, and it's in those places that you experience a deep, internal struggle as you attempt to avoid pain at all costs. When life gets complicated, sad, or boring, you quickly escape to things that bring you pleasure, allowing you to avoid the difficult feelings you fear.

Pursuing your need for adventure, happiness, and stimulating experiences costs you the ability to enjoy the present and find satisfaction in what you already have. You may be extremely busy, packing your schedule full of activities and adventures in order to avoid dealing with your internal anxiety, sorrow, and boredom, aiming for fun and stimulation instead. Putting painful things out of your awareness, or reframing suffering into something positive without truly dealing with it, will continue to show up in counterproductive ways throughout your life.

You can also struggle in relationships, becoming scattered, uncommitted, and unreliable. People close to you can feel frustrated if you value new experiences and things more than them. They can also feel frustrated if you are unwilling to have relational depth, which often requires dealing with challenging emotions and pain.

However, when your heart aligns with the gospel, you become more grounded in the present moment and able to savor it with a grateful heart. Trusting that God will fulfill your internal longings, you find that your grateful, receptive, and thoughtful qualities emerge. Mixed with your natural creativity and energy to inspire others, you bring joy to the sorrows and challenges of life.

TYPE 7

Primary Perspective

- You are convinced you are "allergic" to anything that resembles pain, sadness, grief, boredom, negativity, anxiety, or emptiness.
- You believe if you experience any of these, you will have an "anaphylaxis" reaction that will cause you great harm.
- Therefore, you have perfected the art of escaping these experiences by focusing on and pursuing anything that is new, fun, exciting, entertaining, and stimulating, which fills you with complete satisfaction.

Core Motivations

Core Fear: Being deprived, trapped in emotional pain, limited, or bored; missing out on something fun.
Core Desire: Being happy, fully satisfied, and content.

Core Weakness: Gluttony— Feeling a great emptiness inside and having an insatiable desire to "fill yourself up" with experiences and stimulation in hopes of feeling completely satisfied and content.
Core Longing: "You will be taken care of."

Childhood Patterns

Childhood Message: "It's not okay to depend on others for anything."

Message Your Heart Longs to Hear (Core Longing): "You will be taken care of."

The Type 7 as a Child

You were constantly moving toward excitement, thrills, positivity, and fun in order to avoid anything unpleasant (including boring chores or punishment from parents/authorities). Feeling extremely disappointed and upset when your desires and dreams were shot down, you decided to escape into a more fun and exciting life. You felt frustrated because your deep desires for fun and stimulation were not fully being met, so you decided to rely only on yourself for these things. You knew what you wanted and set out to get it and experience it to make yourself happy and satisfied.

TYPE 7

Wings

Type 7 Wing 6 (7w6)
"The Entertainer"

- **In General:** Outgoing, creative, silly, and playful; cares about what others think and desires to enjoy experiences with others.
- **When Struggling:** Less focused and more revved up and scattered; desires to acquire more relationships and possessions to distract from internal anxieties.
- **Both Types Are in Conflict with Each Other:** The Type 7 is looking for positive and stimulating experiences and freedom, while the Type 6 is focused on establishing supportive relationships and aligning with trusted people.
- **Inspiring Quality:** A committed, loyal, and faithful friend, you bring a lot of fun, joy, and passion to a relationship.

Type 7 Wing 8 (7w8)
"The Realist"

- **In General:** Assertive, confident, ambitious, persistent, and tenacious, with a quick mind and intense energy; less concerned with what others think than the 7w6.
- **When Struggling:** More direct and demanding; workaholic, adrenaline seeker; strategic in getting what they want and aggressive with those who stand in their way.
- **Both Types Blend Easily with Each Other:** Both are aggressive types, making for an aggressive subtype that demands and controls their environment to come through for them (can be mistyped as a Type 8).
- **Inspiring Quality:** Confident and intense with an innovative spirit to overcome any obstacle, you don't see "failure" but an opportunity to see things from a different perspective and try again.

Stress and Growth Paths

Stress | Type 7 moves toward Average to Unhealthy Type 1

- You suddenly become perfectionistic and critical, seeing all the imperfections and wanting them fixed immediately.
- You get frustrated and upset with others who are preventing fun.

Growth | Type 7 moves toward Healthy side of Type 5

- You become grounded, focused, and profound, valuing wisdom and discipline.
- You become more accepting of all of life: good and bad, happy and sad.

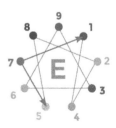

TYPE 7

Levels of Alignment with the Gospel

Aligned (Living as His Beloved)
- Enjoying Christ's blessings that fill you up with great and lasting satisfaction.
- Staying in the present moment and savoring the blessings Christ has given you, which produce gratitude and a content heart.
- Resting in this deeply gratifying place, you are dealing with sadness and disappointment with Christ's strength.
- Remaining playful and fun but becoming principled, practical, focused, and grounded.

Misaligned (Living in Our Own Strength)
- Rejecting any pain, sadness, or disappointment.
- Creating new and exciting experiences to avoid feeling any discomfort when no longer experiencing deep satisfaction in Christ.
- Reframing and convincing yourself and others of a silver lining even when there isn't one, because being fully present in a sorrowful or painful moment is too difficult for you.
- Finding it difficult to focus on projects, commit to relationships, and finish tasks.
- Fleeing and escaping from all problems and negative experiences, which only intensifies the problems.

Out of Alignment (Living as an Orphan)
- Focusing entirely on escaping anything that is causing you pain or boredom.
- Feeling others are keeping you from joy and happiness but failing to see that your insatiable appetites cannot be quenched with earthly pleasures.
- Rejecting any restrictions or limitations placed on you; escaping to anything pleasurable (even if it is risky or bad for you).
- Taking more risks, becoming reckless and prone to addiction.

TYPE 7

Instead of living in bondage to novelty, surrender to the Holy Spirit and depend on him completely, and he will align you with the gospel, where you'll find true freedom and rest.

Communication Style
Brainstorming | Quick | Future Thinking | Storytelling

Your Communication Tendencies

When you are doing well, you speak in a fun, lively, light-hearted, upbeat, optimistic, and joyful way. You also take the time to listen to others without taking over the conversation.

When you are NOT doing well, you can be hyper and scattered, keeping attention on yourself by telling long and grand stories, reframing anything negative, and avoiding anything pessimistic or too deep. If circumstances remain negative, you will feel the need to escape, causing problems in relationships with those who want to work through issues.

Growth Areas for a Type 7's Communication Style
- Be more intentional in your conversations by slowing down, listening to others, and being more serious, thoughtful, and engaging rather than reframing or avoiding what needs to be worked out.
- Remember that others are typically not as quick of a thinker as you.
- Process what needs to be said before you say it so you can deliver it more effectively.

Conflict Style

Common Conflict Activators
- Being limited, restrained, dismissed, or not taken seriously
- Being required to do mundane tasks
- Being unjustly criticized
- Being forced to deal with negative circumstances that might not get resolved
- Being with pessimistic or overly critical people who are always pointing out the negative

Growth Areas for a Type 7's Conflict Style
- Acknowledge that life and conversations cannot always be fun and stimulating.
- Ask God to enable you to work through painful conversations without reframing or escaping.
- Remain focused and committed to resolving the conflict instead of fleeing. This will demonstrate your care for the other person and desire to resolve the issue.
- Offer affirmation and encouragement instead of criticism or condemnation.

Gospel Transformation

Christ Satisfies Your Core Longing

You long to hear, "You will be taken care of," yet no matter how much people try to satisfy this longing, they cannot. But Christ did and did so specifically for you as a Type 7 in these ways:

1. **Complete satisfaction and a content heart is fully yours in Jesus Christ, who is your portion and fill:** We all have a void inside that needs to be filled. Christ is our stream of living water that never runs dry and is always satisfying. As his beloved child, you can enjoy as much living water as you need.

2. **Your needs will be taken care of:** Christ knew that neither others nor you could take care of all your real needs, so he came to earth to take care of all your needs. Rely on his provision for you!

Growth Path for the Type 7

- Observe how often you plan for new experiences and exciting stimulation throughout a day and note any patterns.
- Try to spend time slowing down, processing your feelings, and giving any and all anxieties to Christ to handle.
- Spend intimate time with Christ that remains true to you as a Type 7. Make it exciting, fun, and playful, but be intentional and focused, and savor the time.
- Develop this relationship with Christ; it alone will give you what you are craving. Christ will bring full satisfaction and not disappoint you.
- Focus and listen intently before sharing yourself when you are talking with others. As a Seven, you tend to monopolize conversations. By listening to others, you are showing how they, too, are interesting.
- See God in your everyday experiences and savor him and the life he has given you.

TYPE 7

Understanding Them

Helpful Insight to Understand a Type 7

Just like everyone else, Sevens are prone to the more difficult emotions: anxiety, depression, sadness, loneliness, and frustration. But others don't see them, because Sevens are great at convincing others (and themselves) they are always "on top of the world."

When their darker emotions bring them down, they prefer to experience them alone. They will struggle privately with self-doubt, sadness, loneliness, and even depression.

Sevens are constantly battling the anxiety that they will never really get what they want and need in life and will always feel a deep emptiness inside. To distract themselves from anxieties, they settle for any stimulation or experience.

Recognize Behavior Tendencies When a Type 7 is Activated

An activated Type 7 can:
- Avoid unpleasant situations by thinking and planning for more pleasurable alternatives.
- Rationalize their behavior.
- Reframe circumstances so they sound better to themselves and to others.
- Blame others for being negative and keeping them from having fun.

Ways to Improve Communication with a Type 7 Spouse
- Bid for their attention in an environment that is not too distracting to them.
- Try to bring any negative perspective or disposition back to neutral so as not to activate the Seven's reframing strategies.
- Bring in positive and affirming information before discussing information that might be more negative or difficult for a Seven to hear.
- Incorporate the Seven's ideas into solving problems and give them as much control of the solution and outcome as possible.

How to Relate to a Type 7 in Conflict
- Schedule discussions when you can bring a creative and transcending demeanor instead of an angry, negative attitude.
- Employ positivity, affirmation, and ideas to solve the issue in an upbeat way.
- Allow the Seven to say what they need to say without fear of being punished or trapped in long, negative conversations.

TYPE 7

- Reduce the Seven's impulse to leave a conversation by remaining upbeat and open to creative solutions that fit everyone rather than delivering negative feedback directly to the Seven.

Type 7s Are at Their Best When They:
- Realize setting priorities and limitations will make them more productive and fulfilled.
- Experience a rich and satisfying relationship with Christ.
- Remain focused, steady, grounded, and dependable.
- Control their desires and examine their inner world without needing to flee.
- Embrace the reality of life, facing its sadness, disappointment, and sorrow.
- Become awed by and grateful for the simple wonders of life.
- Are filled with wonder and excitement about experiencing the joys of everyday life.

Affirm Your Type 7 Spouse When They
- Keep their focus on you and fully listen to you.
- Remain in a difficult conversation and express painful emotions.
- Find full satisfaction in Christ rather than experiences.
- Trust Christ to take care of their needs without escaping difficulties.

How to Love Your Type 7 Better
- Share stimulating conversation, laughter, fun, and spontaneous activities when possible.
- Listen patiently to their grand visions and stories without shutting them down.
- Be creative when asking them to do something; they dislike mundane and boring tasks. Make them interesting and fun.
- Be encouraging and positive even when giving them feedback, as criticism can be very painful, discouraging, and deflating for them.
- Give them lots of space, independence, encouragement, and optimistic viewpoints.
- Remind them that God is their Spring of Living Water that never runs out.
- Encourage them to savor the present moment with an observant and grateful heart.

TYPE 7

Type 8: The Protective Challenger

Assertive | Self-Confident | Intense | Big-Hearted | Confrontational

Understanding Me

Summary of Type 8: The Protective Challenger is assertive, self-confident, intense, big-hearted, confrontational.

You engage life with a confident intensity, strength, and determination to make things happen. Your decisive and assertive leadership style causes you to be a powerful change agent in the world, especially when seeking justice and protection for people who can't advocate for themselves.

However, in our world of sin and injustice, people take advantage of others and you feel an intense need to protect yourself against betrayal and powerlessness. You maintain an invincible exterior to minimize dependency and personal exposure.

Your fear of weakness and vulnerability, joined with your thirst for control, power, and justice, can lead you to be too confrontational, domineering, insensitive, and even vengeful, apart from Christ. You attempt to provide protection for yourself by living with a thick piece of steel over your heart, since your heart is extremely tender. But don't misunderstand that strength, because behind it is fear. If other Types fear people and become passive, you fear people and become aggressive. Out of your fear of betrayal you think, "I'll control you before you can control me."

Inevitably, this self-protection ends up doing more harm than good. To protect yourself, you live in denial of any emotions that cause you to feel vulnerable, out of control, and harmed. You live as though your weaknesses never existed.

In relationships with others, you can end up sacrificing intimacy so that your vulnerability won't be discovered and used against you. However, denying yourself closeness, the giving and receiving of forgiveness, and experiencing tenderness leaves you incomplete and unable to experience the intimacy and support you were created to enjoy.

But when your heart is aligned with the gospel and you surrender your fear of betrayal by relying on Christ, you can relinquish your need for control and allow others to see an endearing vulnerability and compassionate strength within you. From that place, you can better protect the innocent from injustice, empower others, and put your strength of leadership to use for the greater good.

Primary Perspective

- You do not want to be controlled or harmed or to allow others to have any power over you (physically, emotionally, or financially).
- Therefore, your highest priority is protecting yourself and those closest to you from being blindsided, controlled, harmed, betrayed, and left at the mercy of injustice.
- You do this by putting on a very intimidating, strong, and protective armor that is powerful and controlling. Unfortunately, it inhibits others from seeing your very tender heart.
- You also don't back down when you desire something. You can persuasively convince others to give you what you want.

Core Motivations

Core Fear: Being weak, powerless, harmed, controlled, vulnerable, manipulated, and left at the mercy of injustice.
Core Desire: Protecting yourself and those in your inner circle.

Core Weakness: *Lust/Excess—* Constantly desiring intensity, control, and power; pushing yourself willfully on life and people in order to get what you desire.
Core Longing: "You will not be betrayed."

Childhood Patterns

Childhood Message: "It's not okay to trust or be vulnerable with anyone."

Message Your Heart Longs to Hear (Core Longing):
"You will not be betrayed."

The Type 8 as a Child

Experiencing harm or betrayal of some kind (or seeing this occur to someone close to you) was the motivating factor for you to put on a thick, strong armor to cover and protect your tender heart from ever being vulnerable again. This armor made you tough, determined, direct, impactful, and action-oriented as a kid. Strong-willed, excessive, impulsive, and willful, you overwhelmed your parents and authority figures. If you felt strongly about something, you'd voice it directly and would not back down. You felt you needed to become an adult at an early age to protect the family or provide in some way.

Wings

Type 8 Wing 7 (8w7) "The Maverick"

- **In General:** Blunt, intense, and demanding; no shortage of energy, tenacity, perseverance, and confidence; insists on others being direct, quick, and assertive.
- **When Struggling:** More focused on gaining power and control; impatient, demanding, impulsive, and lacking compassion for how others feel.
- **Both Types Blend Easily with Each Other:** Produce a very confident, aggressive, and assertive subtype. The Eight wants power, control, and autonomy, and the Seven wants experiences, possessions, and freedom.
- **Inspiring Quality:** A powerful driving force that sees what can and needs to be done and actively gets involved to plow a path for the benefit of others.

Type 8 Wing 9 (8w9) "The Bear"

- **In General:** Steady, patient, compassionate, tender, and soft-hearted when interacting with others; less overtly aggressive, holding power and strength within until it is needed and desiring more comfort and peace.
- **When Struggling:** More intimidating with an unpredictable temper; aggressiveness, control, and demands come out at work, while passivity and accommodation remain at home.
- **Both Types Are in Conflict with Each Other:** The Type 8 is aggressive, assertive, and sure; moves towards conflicts. The passive Type 9 avoids conflicts and upsetting others.
- **Inspiring Quality:** Your gentle strength motivates and inspires others to excel in their particular areas of strength.

Stress and Growth Paths

Stress | Type 8 moves toward Average to Unhealthy Type 5
- You withdraw and observe, becoming secretive when feeling threatened.
- You detach from your emotions and gain more knowledge to get back on the offensive position again when fearing others will betray you.

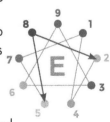

Growth | Type 8 moves toward Healthy side of Type 2
- You're more open-hearted, thoughtful, empathetic, caring, and compassionate as you begin to plow a helpful path for others.
- You open up to others and reveal your vulnerable side.

TYPE 8

Levels of Alignment with the Gospel

Aligned (Living as His Beloved)
- Using your intensity and power to plow a path for those who cannot plow a path for themselves when aligned with the gospel.
- Knowing and trusting you are protected and safe in Christ.
- Letting your tough exterior come down so others can experience your tender, gentle, and thoughtful side.
- Realizing that being vulnerable and transparent is actually a sign of strength, not weakness.
- Resting in the fact that Christ will never betray or forsake you.

Misaligned (Living in Our Own Strength)
- Using your intensity, strength, and confrontational style to scare off those who are trying to harm you.
- Challenging and intimidating others to bring out the truth.
- Refusing to back down if confronted.
- Disregarding others' feelings; extremely blunt and straightforward.
- Having very little patience. Like the snow plow that plows the snow but also forcefully pushes anything out of its way, you will not hesitate to push those who are slow to get out of the way aside and keep plowing.

Out of Alignment (Living as an Orphan)
- Focusing on protecting yourself from those who threaten you.
- Assuming everyone has an agenda to hurt or control you.
- Planning to control others before they can hurt you.
- Becoming vengeful if betrayed or harmed.
- Plowing intentionally over others you think will harm or control you or your loved ones.
- Taking matters into your own hands.

TYPE 8

Instead of living in bondage to aggression, surrender to the Holy Spirit and depend on him completely, and he will align you with the gospel, where you'll find true freedom and rest.

Communication Style
Honest | Direct | Intense | Commanding

Your Communication Tendencies

When you are doing well, you are a generous and loyal friend. Honest and assertive, you have a confident presence. You protect and stand up for the weak, those you love, and those at the mercy of injustice.

When you are NOT doing well, you can be demanding, insensitive, challenging, quick to anger, too assertive and blunt, and unwilling to see how you are hurting others.

Growth Areas for a Type 8's Communication Style
- Realize that being blunt, raw, honest, and direct can hurt others.
- Be softer and more tactful in how you communicate.
- Smile warmly, be patient with others, and always lead with encouragement.
- Listen to those you trust to gauge your intensity when they inform you that it is best to dial the energy back.

Conflict Style

Common Conflict Activators
- Seeing others refusing to deal directly with issues
- Seeing injustices not being addressed
- Seeing others not taking responsibility for their own behavior and actions
- Seeing others not being truthful, direct, and straightforward
- Being blindsided, betrayed, or manipulated

Growth Areas for a Type 8's Conflict Style
- Realize you can easily place circumstances out of your mind and forget they took place with your defensive mechanism of denial.
- Find someone you truly trust and have them tell you when you're too abrasive and intense.
- Accept the view of someone addressing your intensity instead of arguing, denying, or dismissing it.

TYPE 8

Gospel Transformation

Christ Satisfies Your Core Longing

You long to hear, "You will not be betrayed," yet no matter how much people try to satisfy this longing, they cannot. But Christ did and did so specifically for you as a Type 8 in these ways:

1. **Though we are weak, he is strong and protective, and he completed what he set out to accomplish:** We all fall short of God's glory and desperately need a Savior. We are too weak and frail to save ourselves, but Jesus Christ accomplished for us what we could not.

2. **Christ will neither betray nor forsake you:** We have a true advocate whom we can trust. He took perfect care of us through his life and death, and then through conquering death in his resurrection. Nothing can stop Christ from protecting and providing for you. Rest in his power and strength.

Growth Path for the Type 8

- Rest in Christ's protection. He went to great lengths to bring you to himself, and he is not going to allow anyone or anything to come between you and him now.
- Hang up your armor. Jesus Christ's work on your behalf rescues you from being your own protector, as Christ was and is your true armor. You cannot truly save yourself, but Christ can and did. He even conquered death for you, his beloved child.
- Get in touch with your softer, gentler side, and express it more freely toward others.
- Put a "dimmer" on your intensity energy switch. Try to reduce your intensity several notches (but still being your true self) each week and see how this transforms your relationships.

TYPE 8

Understanding Them

Helpful Insight to Understand a Type 8

Eights want to present themselves as strong, confident, tough, and independent so they won't be harmed. But beneath their strong exterior and layers of armor is a very tender heart. It's so tender that its exposure and harm feels like death to the Eight; therefore, they can't allow this kind of betrayal to happen again.

But deep down, Eights desire someone bigger and stronger than them to protect them, allowing them to relinquish their role of vigilant protector and remove their armor to reveal their tender, gentle, caring side. Those who experience this side of an Eight have the privilege of experiencing something great!

Recognize Behavior Tendencies When a Type 8 is Activated

An activated Eight can:
- Synthesize information quickly and act decisively.
- Feel a surge of anger that feels like fire in the gut, which needs to be expelled immediately.
- Use a variety of strategies to protect themselves from being vulnerable, harmed, or controlled.
- Seek advice from only those they trust.
- Discard those they do not respect.

Ways to Improve Communication with a Type 8 Spouse

- Keep your comments brief, purposeful, clear, and direct.
- Allow the Eight to respond whenever they feel the need, and do not be intimidated by their strong stance. They want you to stand your ground and work through the situation with them.
- Demonstrate that you are loyal and protective of them and will go the extra mile to back them up with help.
- Speak with intention; Eights value honesty and directness.
- Ask the Eight clarifying questions to assess where their heart really is versus incorrectly assuming; their direct and intense communication style doesn't mean they are against you.

How to Relate to a Type 8 in Conflict

- Be brief, purposeful, and direct.
- Stand up for yourself and for them.
- Behave with confidence and strength.
- Look past the strong exterior to see their tender heart.
- Acknowledge how they protect and provide.
- Ask clarifying questions and give them the benefit of the doubt; overly blunt and assertive speech doesn't automatically mean they are angry or attacking you.

Type 8s Are at Their Best When They:

- Embrace generosity and mercy, plowing a path for others with their strength.
- Balance courage and strength with a gentle and humble heart.
- Put themselves in harm's way for the sake of justice.
- Know they are protected and safe in Christ.
- Trust Christ will never betray or forsake them but instead will protect and provide for them.

Affirm Your Type 8 Spouse When They:

- Step back rather than push their way through.
- Display vulnerability.
- Trust Christ will protect and never betray them.
- Use their softer side and change how they communicate to accommodate others' communication style and needs.

How to Love Your Type 8 Better

- Be confident, strong, and direct; stand up for yourself and them.
- Do not gossip about them or betray their trust in any way. They do not give their trust away easily.
- Be vulnerable and open up to them. This helps them to feel safe and open up to you.
- Show them that you see and appreciate their tender and vulnerable side without manipulating them to let their guard down.
- Remind them that Christ was the most betrayed man ever, so he understands what betrayal feels like.
- Encourage them to rest in the protection they have in Christ. He will never forsake or betray them.

TYPE 8

Type 9: The Peaceful Mediator

Thoughtful | Reassuring | Receptive | Accommodating | Resigned

Understanding Me

Summary of Type 9: The Peaceful Mediator is thoughtful, reassuring, receptive, accommodating, resigned.

You are an easygoing, non-judgmental, patient person who longs for harmony with others and your environment. Able to see all points of view, you are a natural peacemaker and agent of reconciliation who brings a sense of calm and empathy wherever you go.

Even though you are an easygoing person, you struggle being in a world that is rife with conflict and discord, which threatens the comfort you crave. Feeling that your responsibility is to ensure people experience peace and everyone is respected and heard, you manage the stress you feel by withdrawing or numbing your feelings, dreams, and desires. You "go along to get along" to avoid the internal or external conflict you are feeling.

When trying to satisfy your longing for harmony, connection, and comfort apart from Christ, you avoid conflict and become indecisive, passive, easily overwhelmed, and numb to your life.

Internally, you struggle to believe that your voice and opinions matter; you forget and belittle yourself. Focusing too much on others, you lose your identity, merging with the thoughts, feelings, and agendas of others to achieve a false harmony. You fall asleep to yourself, yet you often feel internal frustration about being overlooked.

Your attempts for harmony eventually backfire in relationships when the people around you get frustrated by your complacency, stubbornness, emotional unavailability, and passive-aggressive responses. Your attempts to avoid conflict, ironically, create the very conflict you desperately want to avoid.

However, when your heart aligns with the gospel, you come awake to your convictions, feelings, and passions. You believe you matter and you make a difference in this world. You also realize that, for you, true connection comes from being willing to engage in conflict with love and courage knowing that, in Christ, peace will come. You engage more genuinely with people and your own life as you bridge differences, bring people together, and achieve true harmony for yourself and the world.

Primary Perspective

- You believe that your presence, opinions, priorities, desires, and life do not matter much to others and the world.
- You believe you should not assert or promote yourself, so you decide to blend in or stay in the background instead. You do this by being easygoing, flexible, even-tempered, accommodating, and agreeable with life and others.
- Your main desire is to have peace of mind and inner stability; you will do almost anything to obtain it. In fact, you will even lose yourself (your passions, talents, drive, calling, and opinions) to keep the peace.
- You easily see everyone's point of view and merge with others to keep harmony.
- Your growth path is to find your own passion and calling and move full force in that direction with boldness and confidence.

Core Motivations

Core Fear: Being in conflict, tension, or discord; feeling shut out and overlooked; losing connection with others.

Core Desire: Having inner stability and peace of mind.

Core Weakness: Sloth— Remaining in an unrealistic and idealistic world in order to keep the peace, remain easy-going and not be disturbed by your anger; falling asleep to your passions, abilities, desires, needs, and worth by merging with others.

Core Longing: "Your presence matters."

Childhood Patterns

Childhood Message: "It's not okay to assert yourself or think much of yourself."

Message Your Heart Longs to Hear (Core Longing): "You presence matters."

The Type 9 as a Child

You strongly felt and identified with the energy, moods, and well-being of your family, so you craved peace and harmony. Any relational tensions overwhelmed you and were extremely uncomfortable for your internal world. It was imperative that you made every effort to keep the peace and create harmony in the family. Your efforts to make others happy led you to merging with others and completely forgetting yourself in the process. You neglected your own desires, passions, and needs in order to accommodate and merge with your family in hopes of bringing harmony. When tensions arose, you would numb out, shut down, withdraw, or disassociate.

TYPE 9

Wings

Type 9 Wing 1 (9w1)
"The Dreamer"

- **In General:** Idealistic, principled, and cerebral; wants to do what is right for everyone; cares about issues of justice, fairness, and people treating one another with kindness and respect.
- **When Struggling:** Quieter and more withdrawn, judgmental, and critical.
- **Both Types Blend Easily with Each Other:** Both types will suppress emotion to maintain peace (Type 9) and sustain self-control (Type 1). You have a friendly, gentle, and encouraging demeanor (Type 9) with perfectionistic tendencies (Type 1).
- **Inspiring Quality:** You make a great mediator with the Nine's ability to see all perspectives from a nonjudgmental posture and the One's insistence on truth, objectivity, and fairness in all circumstances.

Type 9 Wing 8 (9w8)
"The Comfort Seeker"

- **In General:** Sociable, engaging, encouraging, expressive, independent, and assertive; seeks and enjoys comfort more than the 9w1.
- **When Struggling:** More prone to a powerful temper when pushed too far, overlooked, or disrespected, or when others are being mistreated.
- **Both Types Are in Conflict with Each Other:** The Type 9 wants peace and harmony, while the Type 8 brings some aggressiveness, assertiveness, and slight intensity to the laid-back Nine.
- **Inspiring Quality:** Gentle yet powerful, you will assert yourself on behalf of others so they are valued and seen.

Stress and Growth Paths

Stress | Type 9 moves toward Average to Unhealthy Type 6
- Your mind races with possible worst-case scenarios, producing anxiety, worry, irritability and a frantic mind.
- You become irritable, frustrated, reactive, and defensive.

Growth |Type 9 moves toward Healthy side of Type 3
- You become more self-developing, assertive, confident, and energetic.
- You learn that the peace you seek actually comes from showing up, asserting yourself, and blessing others with your full presence.

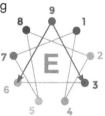

Levels of Alignment with the Gospel

Aligned (Living as His Beloved)

- Awakening to yourself (your passions, likes, dreams, desires, and calling).
- Believing your voice and presence matter to God, others, and the world.
- Honoring yourself by taking the time to know what you want and speak up for yourself.
- Investing in developing yourself, knowing that God has uniquely blessed you with talents and gifts.
- Moving forward with boldness and assertiveness, knowing that your calling and passions will benefit others and glorify God.
- Seeing other people's viewpoints easily and bringing harmony to the most unlikely places without merging with other people in the process.
- Having an indomitable spirit, yet still focusing on loving, supporting, and caring for others. Your strength and kindness both inspire and comfort all.

Misaligned (Living in Our Own Strength)

- Forgetting how valuable you are in Christ and believing your presence does not matter.
- Merging with other people's likes, dislikes, opinions, and emotions.
- Seeing others as being more important than you are.
- Hoping others see your value but not seeking to be recognized.
- Leaning heavily on the affirmations of others rather than the truth of who you really are (Christ's beloved child).
- Feeling unimportant and devastated when others do not realize that you are starving for affirmation and reassurance, overlooking you time and time again.

Out of Alignment (Living as an Orphan)

- Constantly focusing on keeping others happy so you can have (what appears to you to be) peace of mind and inner stability.
- Accommodating everyone and losing yourself in the process.
- Merging fully with others and avoiding developing yourself because you don't believe your presence matters to anyone.
- Following more assertive people who tell you how to live, think, and feel.

TYPE 9

Instead of living in bondage to numbness, surrender to the Holy Spirit and depend on him completely, and he will align you with the gospel, where you'll find true freedom and rest.

Communication Style
Encouraging | Approachable | Friendly | Others-Focused

Your Communication Tendencies
When you are doing well, you are kind, receptive, open, nonjudgmental, peaceful, optimistic, warm, and easy to be with; you're a good listener, fully engaged with others and life.

When you are NOT doing well, you can meander in your talk-style because you're unsure of what you think and feel. You can be passive-aggressive, detached, and stubborn, and you avoid conflict by going along to get along. You might say "yes" when you actually want to say "no" for fear of being in a conflict or upsetting someone.

Growth Areas for a Type 9's Communication Style
- Honor how God made you by getting to know yourself and then communicating your desires, wants, and needs in a more concise, clear, assertive and straight-forward manner. You train others to overlook you because you overlook yourself.
- Be aware of overusing affirming language. Encouraging words are important but can lose their impact when overused.
- Communicate what you really want or need; not doing so can harm you and your relationships.

Conflict Style
Common Conflict Activators
- Feeling any disruption in peace or harmony
- Being taken advantage of or told what to do
- Being overlooked or ignored
- Being directly confronted
- Seeing someone being rude, insensitive, or harsh to others

Growth Areas for a Type 9's Conflict Style
- Realize that not all conflict is bad; it can bring about good when done well.
- Improve yourself by listening to feedback, not avoiding it.
- Focus on knowing your perspective (not all perspectives) and directly expressing it.
- Recognize deep frustration (anger) within you and express it more quickly with emotional balance (being assertive, clear, and direct).
- Apologize if you displace your frustration on someone who was not involved in the original conflict that upset you.

Gospel Transformation

Christ Satisfies Your Core Longing

You long to hear, "Your presence matters," yet no matter how much people try to satisfy this longing, they cannot. But Christ did and did so specifically for you as a Type 9 in these ways:

1. **Your presence matters:** You are so important to him that he sent his only son to live a hard life perfectly for you and die on a cross to have an intimate relationship with you. He is calling you to wake up to yourself, show up, and bless the world with your full presence.

2. **Bless others by asserting yourself, voicing your opinions and desires:** You have the unique ability to see all viewpoints, yet he wants you to voice your own thoughts, feelings, and opinions. By faith, trust God has given you an important voice. Assert yourself in life so everyone can be blessed hearing your viewpoint!

Growth Path for the Type 9

- Express godly confidence in the fact that you matter greatly to Christ and he is calling you to show up in life and bless others with your full presence, voice, and abilities. Do not hoard or hide them; bless others with them!
- Honor God by waking up to your true self and courageously and boldly moving forward in your true calling. Christ created you to have your own unique passions, opinions, and desires to glorify him and bless others.
- Say "no" boldly without needing to excuse yourself.
- Step bravely in the direction where you feel called with action and purpose, knowing God will meet you there.
- Respect yourself in pursuing your calling and passions, even though others will push back when you first begin. Remain steadfast.
- Spend time reading and learning what it means to be God's beloved child so you can truly see and believe how much he cherishes you!
- Practice sharing your thoughts, opinions, and desires with others. Do not be afraid or shy. You matter!

TYPE 9

Understanding Them

Helpful Insight to Understand a Type 9

Appearing easygoing, pleasant, calm, and always willing to accommodate without strong preferences of their own hides the fact that Nines want independence and autonomy (not to be bothered). If life or people interrupt their calm and peaceful state, they will try to accommodate to keep the peace so they can quickly go back to their inner calm. If they are constantly bothered or expected to accommodate, they will become irritated and resentful. They will not express their desires or feelings because they believe it will cause conflicts and discord, so they suppress their anger and simply "go along to get along." They may eventually explode if others constantly demand of them and do not allow them to go back to their inner calm.

Nines need to learn how to express their desires and ask for what they need instead of ignoring their needs or being passive-aggressive about them. Take the time to see if they are feeling internal pressure to accommodate and invite them to share what they really want. Be patient, because assertiveness is scary and difficult for them.

Recognize Behavior Tendencies When a Type 9 is Activated

An activated Type 9 can:

- Withdraw and say nothing as well as hide how they are feeling inside.
- Show a slight indication of anger in their facial tension.
- Remain unaware of their own anger and strategies to protect themselves.
- Redirect their anger and frustration onto another person who was not involved in the original conflict.

Ways to Improve Communication with a Type 9 Spouse

- Develop a safe and warm connection with the Nine before any difficult discussions.
- Invite them to participate in the problem-solving process by letting them know you want to hear from them.
- Help the Nine to feel comfortable, inspired, and excited to make a change. Pressuring them to be quick or decisive will only shut them down. Be patient, kind, and forbearing, like they are to others.
- Encourage and affirm the Nine, which makes them come alive and motivates them to continue being awake, assertive, and confident. You can never genuinely affirm or encourage a Nine enough (not flattery).
- Promote growth by converting negative feedback into a positive path of growth. Criticism and pointing out their faults only make a Nine wither inside.

How to Relate to a Type 9 in Conflict

- Inquire about their frustration (anger) in a kind and receptive manner.
- Remain open; do not pressure them to come through in a specific way.
- Listen fully to them. They can tell when you are not, and it is extremely painful to them.
- Affirm them and cheer them on when they express themselves directly.
- Validate their perspective, especially when you feel you need to share alternative perspectives.
- Demonstrate verbally and nonverbally that their perspective and opinions matter to you.

Type 9s Are at Their Best When They:

- Honor themselves by taking the time to know what they want and then speaking up for themselves with self-confidence.
- Enjoy the peace that comes from Christ, no longer focusing on pleasing people.
- Come fully awake to their abilities, passions, and desires and pursue them; they have a profoundly positive effect on the world.
- Assert themselves instead of giving up their opinions or merging with others. They can accomplish a great deal.
- Know their voice and presence matter to God, others, and the world.

Affirm Your Type 9 Spouse When They:

- Express their desires and passions.
- Assert themselves and do what they want to do.
- Set goals, take a stand on a specific topic, and stand up for their own viewpoints and opinions.
- Trust that their presence and voice matter to Christ and live this out in all areas of their life.

How to Love Your Type 9 Better

- Remind your spouse verbally or nonverbally that their voice and presence matter.
- Demonstrate God's deep love for them by being patient when they are talking and listening to them carefully and with intentionality.
- Give loads of encouragements and affirmations that are specific and thoughtful.
- Encourage them to be bold, strong, and assertive, because God gave them specific attributes to bless others, not to keep to themselves.
- Remind them that they are harming others by not showing up with all they have to offer. Encourage them to bless others with their full presence.
- Remind them often of your love and Christ's love.

TYPE 9

ACKNOWLEDGEMENTS

Our Kids: Nathan and Libby McCord, we are so thankful for each of you, for your kindness, patience, and willingness to embrace what we were learning all these years. You are a true gift and blessing to us.

Our Family: Jerald and Johnny McCord, Dr. Bruce and Dana Pfuetze, Dr. Mark and Mollie Pfuetze. You are all a foundation of love and support, a launching pad for us to live out our calling given to us by God. We respect you and honor you. You have loved us well. Thank you for graciously giving us permission to share our stories so we can help others better understand the power of the Gospel and the impact of the Enneagram.

Our "Your Enneagram Coach" Team: You helped turn our pastoral ministry into a global ministry, bringing the Gospel to thousands. You are a gift from our Father.

Danielle Smith, Christy Knutson, and Jane Butler with Well Refined Co. (along with JoAnna Brown and Madison Church), Traci Lucky, Robert Lewis, and Lindsey Castleman.

Our Friends who have always been near to us: You sat with us in our home, at restaurants, on the phone, allowing us to share what we were learning. You stayed near to us in our darkest seasons when Your Enneagram Coach was born. Your presence in our story is a gift reminding us of our Father's care.

Travis and Susan Stewart, David and Jen Keithley, Dr. Andy and Mandi Mitchell, Tyler and Michelle Kupferschmid, Kyle and Pamela Turner, Robert and Katie Lewis, Matt and Lauren Aiken, Charlie and Tonya Peterson, Chris and Christen O'Cull, Julie Champion, Tiffany Bird, Jeremy and Valerie Brase, Erin MacLean, Bethany Ficks, Jon Bricker, Jeramy and Araya Williams, Annie F. Downs, Matt Ballard, Derek West, Daryl Jones, Rob Sweet, and Eric Hoffman.

Our Friends who have allowed us to share your stories: Thank you for your willingness to be vulnerable and use your experiences to help others. Ken and Jeanette Leggett, Stephanie and Dustin Diez (thanks to Susie Miller for letting us use their story), Karen and Steve Anderson, Dave and Kelsie, Kate and Sam, and Coach Norris. (In some stories, names have been changed but the details are accurate and used with permission.)

Our Mentors: You took to heart Paul's charge to invest in the lives of others so that they too would extend the Gospel to another generation. We pass along to others what you have generously given to us.

Dr. Bob and Karen Smart, Mike and Donna Henry, Rev. Bill and Karen Vogler, Bruce Edstrom, Dr. Dan Zink, Doug and Pam Nuenke.

Our Spiritual Teachers and authors we have learned from: We are so thankful for your books, sermons, messages, and training. May our efforts honor your work.

Dr. Bryan Chapell, Tim Keller, Jack and Rose Marie Miller, Dan Allender, Larry Crabb, Scott Sauls (a special thanks to Scott for writing the Foreword to *Becoming Us*).

Our Enneagram Teachers and Coaches: Thank you for all you have done ahead of us. Katherine Fauvre, Ian Cron, Suzanne Stabile, Ginger Lapid-Bogda, Russ Hudson, Don Riso, Jessica Dibb, Helen Palmer, Dr. David Daniels, Marilyn Vancil, Elizabeth Wagele, David Fauvre, and Chris Heuertz.

Our Business Supporters and Friends: We are so thankful for Michael Hyatt and Co., who not only gave us opportunities to work with your team, but generously shared your insight and resources that helped us to launch Your Enneagram Coach.

Michael and Gail Hyatt, Joel and Megan Miller, Suzie and Justin Barbour, Mandi Rivieccio, Mandy Raff, and the rest of the Michael Hyatt & Co. team.

Our Publisher: Morgan James Publishing, David Hancock, Karen Anderson, Jim Howard, Aubrey Kincaid, thank you for your encouragement and commitment to publish a book that best represents our message and serves our audience. We have enjoyed working with each of you.

Our Writing Team at StrategicBookCoach.com who helped us write the book: When our Father put before us an opportunity to put our experience and insight into a book, we cried out to him for help. It is true, we can do all things through Christ when he provides us with a team like you all. Thank you, Karen Anderson, for your endless help, guidance, care, support, and wisdom. Without you this book would not be possible. We are also grateful for your team, Sharilyn Grayson and Sissi Haner.

Our Church Family: Thank you for all your love and support for us in our journey. Southpointe Community Church, Nashville, Tennessee, and Christ Church in Normal, Illinois.

Music that has touched our hearts: Indelible Grace for their redone hymns; Sleeping at Last for their Enneagram songs and instrumental music.

We are incredibly blessed to have so many people God has used to come alongside us in our journey. Even if we didn't mention you by name, please know we are beyond grateful for you in our lives. Thanks to all who have loved us so well.

About the Authors

Beth McCord is the Founder and Lead Content Creator of Your Enneagram Coach (.com), a Certified Enneagram Coach, and has been using the Enneagram in ministry since 2002. She has been featured in articles for *Relevant* magazine and other faith-based magazines, been a featured expert on many podcasts, and is a frequent speaker on the Enneagram.

Jeff McCord is Executive Director of Your Enneagram Coach, a Certified Enneagram Coach, a Certified Conciliator with the Institute of Christian Conciliation, and a practicing Family Mediator. He has also served as a pastor in the Presbyterian Church in America congregation for the last twenty years.

Beth and Jeff McCord have helped over 250,000 people to discover their unique personality Type and apply that knowledge to their relationships. With twenty-four years' experience in ministry, they are the founders of **YourEnneagramCoach.com**, an organization offering Gospel-centered Enneagram courses and coaching.

The McCords live in Franklin, Tennessee, with their blue-eyed Australian Shepherd dog, Sky.

BECOME YOUR BEST SELF WITH THE ENNEAGRAM.

TYPE-SPECIFIC ONLINE COURSES • LIVE EVENTS • PERSONAL COACHING

erything we do at Your Enneagram Coach is aimed to help you see yourself with
tonishing clarity so you can break-free from self-condemnation, fear and shame
knowing and experiencing unconditional love, forgiveness and freedom in Christ.

u deserve to live the life you were created to live. *We'll help you get there.*

NFIRM YOUR TYPE AT YOURENNEAGRAMCOACH.COM

Your
Enneagram
Coach

REFERENCES

The Enneagram is a very old typology, and many people over the years have helped it to become useful today. Because the Enneagram itself has been around for ages, many terms are common usage in the Enneagram world. If at all possible, we give credit to those whose ideas have influenced us. For all these people, we are grateful.

The Enneagram Institute

Riso, Don Richard. *Discovering Your Personality Type: The New Enneagram Questionnaire.* Boston: Houghton Mifflin, 1995.

Riso, Don Richard. Enneagram *Transformations: Releases and Affirmations for Healing Your Personality Type.* Boston: Houghton Mifflin, 1993.

Riso, Don Richard, and Russ Hudson. *The Wisdom of the Enneagram: The Complete Guide to Psychological and Spiritual Growth for the Nine Personality Types.* New York: Bantam, 1999.

Riso, Don Richard, and Russ Hudson. *Personality Types: Using the Enneagram for Self-Discovery.* Boston: Houghton Mifflin, 1987.

Riso, Don Richard, and Russ Hudson. *Understanding the Enneagram: The Practical Guide to Personality Types.* Boston: Houghton Mifflin, 1990.

Enneagram Introductions

Baron, Renee, and Elizabeth Wagele. *The Enneagram Made Easy: Discover the 9 Types of People*. San Francisco: Harper San Francisco, 1994.

Cron, Ian Morgan, and Suzanne Stabile. *The Road Back to You: An Enneagram Journey to Self-Discovery*. Downers Grove, IL: IVP, an Imprint of InterVarsity, 2016.

Stabile, Suzanne. *The Path Between Us*. Downers Grove, IL: IVP, an Imprint of InterVarsity, 2018.

Narrative Tradition

Daniels, David N., and Virginia Price. *The Essential Enneagram: The Definitive Personality Test and Self-Discovery Guide*. San Francisco: Harper San Francisco, 2000.

Palmer, Helen. *The Enneagram: Understanding Yourself and the Others in Your Life*. San Francisco: Harper San Francisco, 1991.

Christian Perspective

Rohr, Richard, Andreas Ebert, and Peter Heinegg. *The Enneagram: A Christian Perspective*. New York: Crossroad Pub, 2001.

Sherrill, AJ. *Enneagram and the Way of Jesus: Integrating Personality Theory with Spiritual Practices and Biblical Narratives*. CreateSpace Independent Publishing Platform, 2016.

Vancil, Marilyn. *Self to Lose—Self to Find: A Biblical Approach to the 9 Enneagram Types*. Enumclaw, WA: Redemption Press, 2016.

Advanced Enneagram Studies

Bartlett, Carolyn. *The Enneagram Field Guide: Notes on Using the Enneagram in Counseling, Therapy, and Personal Growth*. Nine Gates Publishing, 2007.

Bast, Mary, and Thomson, Clarence. *Out of the Box: Coaching with the Enneagram*. Louisburg, KS: Ninestar Publishing, 2005.

Chestnut, Beatrice. *The Complete Enneagram: 27 Paths to Greater Self-Knowledge*. Berkeley, CA: She Writes Press, 2013.

Flaherty, James. *Coaching: Evoking Excellence in Others*. Boston: Butterworth-Heinemann, 1999.

Palmer, Helen. *The Enneagram in Love and Work: Understanding Your Intimate and Business Relationships*. San Francisco: HarperOne, 1995.

Enneagram in Business

Lapid-Bogda, Ginger. *Bringing out the Best in Yourself at Work: How to Use the Enneagram System for Success*. New York: McGraw-Hill, 2004.

Lapid-Bogda, Ginger. *The Enneagram Development Guide*. Santa Monica, CA: Enneagram in Business, 2011.

Lapid-Bogda, Ginger. *What Type of Leader Are You?: Using the Enneagram System to Identify and Grow Your Leadership Strengths and Achieve Maximum Success*. New York: McGraw-Hill, 2007.

Enneagram in Parenting

Levine, J. *Know Your Parenting Personality: How to Use the Enneagram to Become the Best Parent You Can Be*. Hoboken, NJ: John Wiley & Sons, 2003.

Wagele, Elizabeth. *The Enneagram of Parenting: The 9 Types of Children and How to Raise Them Successfully*. New York: HarperOne, 1997.

Resources

Allender, Dan B. *The Healing Path: How the Hurts in Your Past Can Lead You to a More Abundant Life*. Walker Large Print, 2003.

Allender, Dan B., and Tremper Longman. *Intimate Allies: Rediscovering God's Design for Marriage and Becoming Soul Mates for Life*. Tyndale House Publishers, Inc., 1995.

Benson, Kyle. "The #1 Thing Couples Fight About." The Gottman Institute, August 5, 2016. https://www.gottman.com/blog/one-thing-couples-fight-about/

Bridges, Jerry. *The Discipline of Grace: God's Role and Our Role in the Pursuit of Holiness*. NavPress, 2006.

Bridges, Jerry. *Transforming Grace*. NavPress, 2017.

Bridges, Jerry, and Jerry Bridges. *Trusting God*. NavPress, 2016.

Chandler, Matt. *Recovering Redemption: How Christ Changes Everything*. LifeWay Press, 2014.

Chapell, Bryan. *Holiness by Grace: Delighting in the Joy That Is Our Strength*. Crossway Books, 2011.

Chapell, Bryan, and Kathy Chapell. *Each for the Other: Marriage as It's Meant to Be*. Baker Books, 2006.

Crabb, Larry. *Connecting: Healing Ourselves and Our Relationships*. Thomas Nelson, 2005.

Crabb, Larry. *Fully Alive: A Biblical Vision of Gender That Frees Men and Women to Live beyond Stereotypes*. Baker Books, 2014.

Crabb, Larry. *Inside Out*. NavPress, 2013.

Crabb, Larry. *The Pressure's Off: Breaking Free from Rules and Performance*. Waterbrook Press, 2012.

Esfahani-Smith, Emily. "Masters of Love." *The Atlantic*, June 12, 2014. https://www.theatlantic.com/health/archive/2014/06/happily-ever-after/372573/

Gottman, John M., and Joan DeClaire. *The Relationship Cure: A Five-Step Guide to Strengthening Your Marriage, Family, and Friendships*. Harmony Books, 2002.

Gottman, John Mordechai, and Nan Silver. *The Seven Principles for Making Marriage Work*. Seven Dials, an Imprint of Orion Publishing Group Ltd., 2018.

Horton, Michael Scott. *Putting Amazing Back into Grace*. Hodder & Stoughton, 1996.

Johnson, Sue. *Hold Me Tight: Your Guide to the Most Successful Approach to Building Loving Relationships*. Piatkus, 2011.

Keller, Timothy, and Kathy Keller. *The Meaning of Marriage: Facing the Complexities of Commitment with the Wisdom of God*. Hodder & Stoughton, 2013.

Keller, Timothy, Michael Horton, and Dane Calvin Ortlund. *Shaped by the Gospel: Doing Balanced, Gospel-Centered Ministry in Your City: A New Edition of Section One of Center Church*. Zondervan, Redeemer City to City, 2016.

Manning, Brennan, and Jon Foreman. *Abba's Child: The Cry of the Heart for Intimate Belonging*. NavPress, 2015.

Miller, Susie. *Listen, Learn, Love: How to Dramatically Improve Your Relationships in 30 Days or Less!* Dunham Books, 2015.

Murray, John. *Redemption Accomplished and Applied*. William B. Eerdmans Publishing Company, 2015.

Piper, John. *The Purifying Power of Living by Faith in Future Grace*. Multnomah Press, 1995.

Sande, Ken. *The Peacemaker: A Biblical Guide to Resolving Personal Conflict*. Baker Books, 2004.

Sauls, Scott. *Jesus Outside the Lines: A Way Forward for Those Who Are Tired of Taking Sides*. Tyndale House Publishers, 2015.

Sauls, Scott. *From Weakness to Strength: 8 Vulnerabilities That Can Bring Out the Best in Your Leadership*. David C. Cook, 2017.

Smart, Robert Davis. *Embracing Your Identity in Christ: Renouncing Lies and Foolish Strategies*. WestBow Press, 2017.

Ward, Tyler. *Marriage Rebranded*. Moody Publishers, 2014.